A Breath of
Moonscent

A Memoir of a Devon Childhood

A Breath of Moonscent

A Memoir of a Devon Childhood

by

Allan Boxall

BLUE POPPY PUBLISHING

Transcription by Sarah Boxall
Edited by Sarah Dawes
Cover art by Sarah Lannigan
Cover design by Oliver Tooley

Blue Poppy Publishing

Devon EX34 9HG

info@bluepoppypublishing.co.uk

ISBN-13 978-1-911438-60-1

FOREWORD

By Liz Shakespeare

North Devon holds a special place in many people's hearts. It is an area of deep winding lanes, steeply wooded coombes and secluded streams, ancient farmhouses nestling amongst undulating patchworks of small fields and high hedges, with church towers on the skyline and distant views of moorland. For centuries it was difficult for travellers to access, being far from main roads and bordered by the inhospitable terrain of Exmoor to the northeast, Dartmoor to the south, and by the sea to the west. The ancient landscape was secluded and individual, causing its people to be wary of strangers, self-reliant and resistant to change. Most people could trace their families back for many generations, and even in the mid-twentieth century there were few newcomers, so traditions persisted here that had died out in most areas of the country. Remote farms and hamlets were somewhat dishevelled; ready cash was in short supply and, in any case, appearances counted for little. Usefulness was paramount. Why replace a ramshackle barn built from crumbling cob and rusting corrugated iron, as long as it continued to serve its purpose? There were no manicured villages in North Devon then; it was a different place from today. I remember it well, and in many ways regret its passing.

There have been few authors who have known North Devon well enough to write about it convincingly; Henry Williamson, Ronald Duncan and Ted Hughes are among the exceptions. I was, therefore, delighted when *A Breath of Moonscent* was sent to me. Allan Boxall has a deep understanding of North Devon that can be gained only through long acquaintance. He came to know the landscape through exploration of every field, lane and wood as a boy; its people through living in close proximity.

A Breath of Moonscent focusses on an area of North Devon that has been lovingly documented before, but not in words. The Dolton area was the subject of much work by the eminent photographer James Ravilious, who worked for the Beaford Photographic Archive for seventeen years, creating an invaluable record of rural life. The aim of the project was to capture the very special and individual nature of North Devon just as it was starting to change. Allan Boxall's written account depicts the same area at an earlier time, before change was envisaged, and he portrays in words what Ravilious achieved in images.

Allan Boxall moved to North Devon with his parents during the Second World War, when he was four years old. His father was employed as a gardener by a family who, wanting to escape the bombing of southeast England, moved to their country residence in Devon. It was an unfettered childhood; he was free to roam the countryside and get to know its inhabitants, soon making friends and acquiring a Devon accent. Throughout the book the Devon dialect is perfectly conveyed, something which is not easy to achieve in print.

This is not a romanticised account of rural life. There are hardships, there are deaths, there are regrets, but the author shows that these events are part of the natural cycle of life. Even the deaths of his pets take on a universal significance through the perceptive and empathetic way they are described.

Reading his portrayals of the people of Dolton, one feels one has known them personally – or, at least, seen a Ravilious photograph of them.

'Tom Baker was a tough old fellow, gnarled and stringy as a war-scarred tomcat, a face weather-beaten and ravaged by seventy years of sun, rain, and biting winds, pocked by the savage stings of angry wasps which had attacked him when he accidentally hacked into their nest whilst paring a hedge, mean and short-tempered through decades of failed harvests, which he remembered more than the successful ones.

His wife was a little woman, stringy and tough herself, bowed and worn, wrinkled-apple face and age-speckled hands from a lifetime of milking, chicken plucking, rabbit gutting, kitten drowning, and cooking for Tom and their only son, Frank.'

Some of the people Boxall writes about were indeed photographed by Ravilious in later years; Doris Friend, Dennis Harris, Tommy Isaacs and, of course, one of Ravilious's favourite subjects, Archie Parkhouse, who is as familiar from Boxall's description as he is from the photographs.

'A life outdoors had creased his features like tanned leather, hewn his hands gnarled and roughened by toil. He wore a battered and stained trilby above a face eagle-eyed and starkly handsome. His keen eyes sparkled mischievously.'

Until comparatively recent times, life in North Devon was dominated by the seasons and the weather, because most people either worked on the land, or walked or cycled along miles of narrow lanes to reach school or work. Boxall recalls in loving detail the skeletal woods and barren fields of winter, the magical return of spring when 'snowdrops lined the brook like a carpet of green-tinted snow', the summer hedgerows 'awash with summer seas of umbellifers and red campion . . . honey bees and bumble bees, wood wasps and butterflies; a kaleidoscope of pastel colours shimmering and swaying,' and autumn, 'with the beech leaves golden, the oak secreting fawn-brown acorns neat in their pitted cups.' Harvest was a special time which involved most of the local community.

'As the afternoon lengthened, a cheerful team of farm wives would appear with baskets of food – egg and bacon pie, cheese and pickles with home-baked bread, pasties, apple pie with lashings of yellow-crusted clotted cream – and the workers would squat in the shade of the binder or stooks of corn, wipe the engrained sweat from their brows and eat hungrily, chatting between draughts of cider and cold tea.'

Alongside the lyrical descriptions of landscape, there are moments of real hilarity. There is 'the legend of Dennis's boot' which was accidentally thrown in the river, leading to an epic tale of subterfuge and resultant merriment. Also, the account of moving house and the difficulties of descending a steep, stony lane with a china cabinet, Calor gas stove and other household accoutrements piled precariously high on a cart drawn by a horse made excitable by the passing of the hunt.

Boxall has documented a small area of North Devon in intimate and affectionate detail; he knows every inch, having explored the woods, waded through the river, climbed the rocky walls of the quarry and walked the deep, narrow lanes daily alongside his neighbours.

His writing takes us back to a magical era, when life was hard, but the rewards were great. Now, whenever I am out at night in the countryside of North Devon, I will remember his descriptions of the time when there were no sounds of distant traffic, when the stars were brighter, and the silence was disturbed only by the hoot of an owl or the bark of a fox.

Liz Shakespeare

PROLOGUE

The valley lay hidden from the rest of the world in a fold of the Devon countryside. A river flowed along its floor as if once, aeons ago, the river, itself a mighty torrent, had sculpted the valley until, its crafting done, it had receded. Ferns and trees materialised to soften, then cover, the exposed slopes; small mammals arrived, burrowed into the dark soil to build their nests. Wild boar appeared, and bears, to forage the forested slopes and drink from the crystal-clear waters where beavers built their lodges. Birdsong echoed throughout the forest and a wild, yet contented, constancy descended through the millennia. But then had come Man, and the old constancy vanished, its balance marred as he began to pattern the valley in pursuit of his own needs. The great wildwood, dark and tangled, receded diminished, gave way to enclosed fields. Soon only tiny slivers of the old wilderness remained, drawing its ancient secrets into itself.

Throughout the following centuries the river saw numerous people born, live and die, until…

… Just for a while, this is the way it was.

ARRIVAL

Gwen had painted one of the granite bridge stones white so that we wouldn't miss the drive or hit the bridge or plunge into the river. I had heard Dad say this to the driver as we sat wedged, him and my mother, my baby sister asleep on her lap, in the cab of the removal lorry. Once again, the lights had gone out all over Europe, and the darkness enveloped us; only the dipped and shielded headlights lighted the road ahead.

The roads had grown steadily narrower, steeper, since we had left Exeter, until now, as the lorry bumped and rattled in low gear down the hill towards the end of our long journey from Surrey, the hedgerows closed frighteningly in on us. Things clicked and snapped angrily against the lorry sides. A tunnel of trees swallowed us, scritch-scratching the cab roof as if resenting our encroachment upon their domain.

I shrank lower between my parents, watching demon shadows dance in the headlights.

"There it is!" exclaimed Dad.

And, sure enough, there it was, a white stone which flashed dully, briefly, before we turned into the drive. Relief encompassed me. We were going to a new home where Hitler couldn't find us; that terrifying little man with evil black eyes and a dark smudge beneath his nose, who, Mum informed me in the morning after one raid, had broken her favourite vase; just snuck into our house and smashed it out of sheer nastiness, I assumed. There would be no more lunging searchlights and snarling aeroplanes, crumpled shrapnel falling from the sky; no more uncomfortable nights sleeping atop Dad's old tool chest in the Anderson shelter. I was four, nearly five, and for the last two years had been haunted by wailing sirens and the crump of gunfire; a nervous, fear-filled Mum. Once, "They're after Vickers tonight," Dad had said, sounding tense.

The smell of damp and mould, wet sandbags. A torch beam darting claustrophobically around the shelter like a startled spider. Flashes of alarmed voices from somewhere outside.

"Oh, Christ, it's on fire, our house has been hit." Dad dashed from the shelter regardless of danger. "No, thank God, it's the pig shed in the field across the road."

Later, as the all-clear sounded, we stumbled above ground to see the pigsty at the far end of the field had taken a direct hit.

"Poor pigs," said Mum.

"Roast pork," quipped Dad, from sheer relief.

* * * * *

The drive was a mere ribbon of pitted tarmac threading through wooded darkness. The lorry groaned painfully as we climbed suddenly, stars swooped to fill the windscreen as, with a guttural sigh and crunch of gears, we levelled out on a milky plateau.

The engine fell silent and the adults scrambled chattering from the cab. I was lifted and placed down into a silent and alien world of frightening emptiness, under a vault of stars.

And there was the moon! How did it get here? Had it followed us? I was aware of damp grass beneath my feet and reached eagerly for Mum's hand as shapes slowly took form around us; a sequestered valley, deep and mysterious behind which a forest of mercurial darkness rose whispering into the night.

Before I had a chance to make sense of any of this I was led toward a cream-painted cottage, pallid in the moonlight. Around me the grown-ups towered indistinct and comforting, and the backs of my knees ached with growing pains as the cottage door closed upon the night.

* * * * *

The bed felt different and I was confused. Lemon shades danced mischievously behind my eyelids and, when I opened my eyes, sunlight was streaming through a latticed window; I remembered. I blinked a couple of times and sunbeams sprayed off my lashes like dewdrops. There was a sound now, soft and throaty, a gentle sound which rose and fell rhythmically outside the window. I lay, listening. Birdsong rang in silver chimes, sharp and precise as beads of light. Sunbeams danced subdued off saffroned walls, skittered playfully across my eiderdown, and I was overcome by a wave of curiosity.

"Mum!"

Soft tread on the stairs and she appeared in the bedroom doorway, fresh and smiling, and the light bobbed in her russet hair like fiery moths.

* * * * *

Our new home was a lodge in the grounds of a country house of which my father was to be the gardener. Dad was a slight man with a shock of black hair like a violent inky sky above a stern, weathered face. He hadn't wanted to be a gardener. He had wanted to be a soldier, but misshapen fingers on his right hand precluded that ambition. He wouldn't be able to handle a rifle properly, they said. Rubbish, said Dad, he was left-handed, anyway.

Sometimes, back in Surrey, when a martial tune played on the wireless, Dad would grab a broom and march up and down the living room, "Left-right, left-right. Halt!" his voice a cudgel. "About...turn!" Up and down he went, backwards and forwards, his shock of sloe-black hair jumping and trembling, his craggy face brooking no nonsense. "Shoulder...arms! Pre-zent arms!" and the broomstick would slap across and down and rap upon the floor and Mum would smile indulgently while I gazed on in wide-eyed bemusement. Later, in Devon, he was to join the Home Guard and get to handle a rifle proper and learn unarmed combat to tackle any invading Jerries.

But, for now, frustrated, he continued working as a gardener for a successful business family, the Duttons, which had patriotically enlisted in the navy at the outbreak of hostilities, all but the wife, that is, who remained in their Weybridge residence. The younger of the servants – butler, maids, cook – had enlisted too, inaugurated into the armed forces or for essential war work. Only Dad and Gwen, the maid, remained.

"We're moving to Devon," Dad had proclaimed one day in his brook-no-nonsense tone.

Mum gazed, appalled.

"The country residence; Madam's transferring down there for the duration of the war. She's requested me and Gwen go too – you and the kids as well, of course."

"But my family's here, Bill, and yours," Mum protested.

"We'll come back of course, when it's over, and for holidays," said Dad.

"But … Devon, Bill?" Mum had visions of rustics in smocks, buck-toothed simpletons chewing straws who 'ooh-arred' and babbled in an incomprehensible bucolic burr.

"You'll be safe from the air-raids, Eed," said Dad, grinning sardonically. "I can't get you out of the shelter with the children nowadays, every time you hear a plane. Anyway, it's my job." Dad had lived through the depression and had a pathological fear of unemployment and the dole.

And so we had moved. Of Gwen I remember nothing, just her name which echoes down the decades, mainly, I suspect, because later Dad named one of our hens after her. She couldn't have stayed long in Devon. Probably homesick, she had returned to Surrey, preferring the bombs to remoteness and solitude.

DISCOVERY

I was to fall deeply in love with the valley, with its river, its misted solitude and verdant fields, its steeply wooded slopes, scented air, its wildlife and livestock, the scattered farms and cottages and their inhabitants. But on this first morning, as my parents busily furnished our new home and my baby sister slept peacefully, I ventured forth warily into the unknown.

Beyond shrubs now polished sleek and shiny by the risen sun, the Scots pine (I later learned all their names) rose majestically above its deciduous contemporaries. On one of its lower branches I spotted the source of a mysterious sound. A large bird, dusted blue, plump and cosy-looking, bobbed its head, one eye gazing keenly down at me. Its pastelled chest rose and fell and the sound trembled earthwards like cotton wool. Abruptly, with a sharp crack of wings, it became airborne and sped with great velocity towards the misted forest beyond an as yet sunless valley.

Now another sound; a hushed and continuous rushing like static on our wireless when Mum turned the dials. It arose from somewhere deep in this mysterious valley. I became aware of birdsong all around me, sharp and rapturous like fluted dreams.

As the sun rose higher, gold trickled down the slopes of the distant forest, dissipating the mist. It hit the valley bed, unrolling the carpet of darkness to reveal a verdant meadowland. I turned to where a grand sweep of lawn sported coloured teardrops, carelessly shed, blue and white. At the apex of the lawn the big house stood grandiosely against the sky. Latticed windows gazed coolly at me, neat thatch worn like a protective sunhat. Hesitantly I approached it.

The world sang and I was alive and drowning in wonder. The grass felt spongy, friendly beneath my tread. I saw now that the gaudy teardrops were flowers of some kind, spearing from the green earth. The big house frowned haughtily at me, indignant as I stopped to pluck one of its bejewelled flowers, close enough to smell the earthy fragrance of new birth before I toddled eagerly home with it.

It was a crocus, Dad informed me. He frowned. And I wasn't to pick any more.

The plump bird was a woodpigeon, he said; not a gardener's best friend.

I trundled off. Later, as the sun climbed higher, the valley basked in a warm green light and the liquid forest rippled, poised like a threatening wave never to descend.

* * * * *

The days grew longer, warmer. The grass, too, and new-sprung leaves fluttered chattering in the slightest breeze. Birdsong became intense and anticipatory, a cacophony of tumbling harmonics. I spent longer outdoors, becoming increasingly bold, venturing deeper into the copse across the drive where the Scots pine grew, snowy clouds in haughty silence high above its uppermost tip. Beneath my feet last autumn's leaves crackled like breakfast cereal. Stray twigs brushed against my legs. The breeze created an overture in the trees, haunting and timeless as I gazed into their depths, and for the first time in my life I experienced solitude and instantly embraced it.

Below me, in the treetops halfway down the valley side, something large and dark moved. The emerald canopy trembled and quavered, and branches crackled as whatever it was lurched ponderously away.

And now I became aware of the abundance of life, semi-concealed and camouflaged, flitting and scuttling, irresolute of form. Airborne insects rose and fell, forming intricate patterns in pillars of dusty sunlight. Between the trees and blue-misted distance I could see the mysterious, sun-darkened forest. At its base an exquisite braid of effervescent gold dipped and flounced in an endless chain, and again I was aware of that ribbon of sound like distant surf, timeless and pervasive.

MR FORD AND PUSS

In the backyard of our lodge stood an elongated shed, probably once a stable but now largely empty, a magnet for my inquisitiveness.

The wooden doors scrunched, growled, and juddered as I opened them. Grey dust rose and dimness leapt out at me. I paused before venturing further. The earthen floor was slightly concave, the one small window grime-encrusted. Old sacks lay mouldering in a corner exuding a pungent musk. A disorderly pile of logs lay against one wall.

Hesitantly I advanced into the shed.

Then froze.

Fear stabbed me in the chest as something large and sinuous flashed from behind the logs to melt into deeper shadow. As I backpedalled fearfully towards the door, two luminous eyes glared at me from a far corner.

"Mum!" I ran stumbling, heart beating fast.

"There's something in the shed, Mum!"

"There is, duck?" She wore a smock over her dress and was kneeling before the fireplace; there was a ladder in one stocking and her slippers were holed.

"Yeah, something … something alive, and it's huge!"

Mum turned her head. A smear of soot angled down one cheek. "I can't just now, duck, I'm -"

"No, now!"

Loose strands of hair coiled over her eyes. "I'm -"

"Now, I said!" I could be a spoilt brat when Dad wasn't around.

Mum sighed defeatedly and rose to her feet, sweeping back the stray hair and smearing further coal over her cheek. She looked flushed. "Alright. Quick, then."

She hesitated at the shed door. "It might be a rat," she said, in sudden alarm. "You shouldn't go in there."

"No … it may be." I wasn't sure what a rat was. "It's got great shiny eyes and it's alive!"

15

"Then it's a rat! You mustn't go in there."

"Bain't no rats een there," came a crackly voice.

We both turned to see an old man with a wrinkly face and twinkly eyes. His dense moustache twitched as he spoke, reminding me of a huge bristly caterpillar. He grinned, exposing tobacco-stained teeth.

"Not wi' thiky cat'n er kittens een there, that's fer zure." He paused. "You must be Bail's missus'n bay."

"Bill, yes." Mum frowned guardedly at him.

"Vrank Vord." The old man extended a brown and gnarled hand.

Mum eyed it suspiciously, finally shook it, then wiped her hand on her apron.

"I wuz gardener yur vore 'twuz zold. Retired now. Just kaipin'n eye on the place, like, 'til Bail gits settled."

"Oh, yes," said Mum. She sounded wary.

"Cat een there wi' er kittens," the old man repeated. He nodded, to confirm it, then said, "Well, I'll be gettin' on 'ome then. Nice to mait ee, Mrs … er."

"Boxall," Mum said.

"Boxall. Right. I'll be gettin' on 'ome then, Mrs Boxall."

Mum gazed contemplatively at his retreating back. After a while, she said, "Must be a yokel," as if referring to some sub-species. "The way he speaks, I wonder he may be a bit simple."

* * * * *

Mr Ford, for that's who the old man was, lived three miles of fields and lanes away from our lodge, in Hill Cottage, perched atop a knoll and separated from the Methodist chapel next door – the only other building there – by a barrier of garden shrubs. Two winding country roads rose to the top of the knoll, intersected, then dropped away again into rolling farmland.

"Saw they furriners up to the lodge today," Mr Ford informed his wife, a little bespectacled old lady with grey hair drawn back in a bun. Wisps of escaped hair haloed ethereally around her head.

"Did ee hever? What be 'em like?" Mrs Ford nodded slightly as she spoke, as if aping an invisible metronome. It made her appear frail.

Gyp, their ageing mongrel dog, gazed up from his blanket by the open fire as if he too were interested. His eyes were doleful, a little clouded now, his muzzle grey; it quivered and drops of saliva traversed his whiskers like dew. He, too, looked frail.

"Bail zeems friendly nuff." Mr Ford nodded sagely. "Ee's missus, er be a bit off though, 'n' they've got a young bay." He paused, stroked his moustache. "Mind you, they all spake vunny, like. Lunnon talk, I s'pose. Quare volk, saims to me."

Gyp dropped his head and closed his eyes. He began to snore.

* * * * *

This interchange was somewhat amusedly hinted at some months later, when Mum, my sister Valerie and I were invited to tea by Mrs Ford.

Hill Cottage held a seductive aroma of fruit cake and clotted cream which blended with warmth from a log fire. Gyp plodded arthritically to investigate us, tail wagging uncertainly, eyes wary. He sniffed each of us tentatively. Reassured, he followed us into the front room where I gazed in awe at a full table of ham, cheese, and egg sandwiches, jam and scones, Victoria sponge oozing jam and dusted with icing sugar, clotted cream thick and farm-fresh with a dimpled yellow crust. A log fire crackled gaily in the grate, cosy and warm, and the sun through the window bathed everything in a golden glow.

Sometimes, on later visits, the wind whistled and probed, and rain drummed on the windowpanes. But the fire just crackled more heartily, flames danced and pirouetted, and Mrs Ford would say, "The days be drawin' een vast, that's fer zure," and she would light the oil lamp. Old Gyp would rise stiffly to his feet, toasted too hot, and waddle under the table from where he would nudge my knees with his chin, soliciting titbits. "Gyp! What be ee 'bout o'," Mrs Ford would exclaim. And Gyp would sink silently to the floor.

On the way home dusk would be approaching. Grass, long in the hedgerows, sighed in the wind. Flocks of crested peewits shimmering purple green sought grubs and insects in ploughed fields, which lay brown and stark under a grey sky. As finally we climbed the rise to Brightley Lodge, stars appeared then vanished, brushed by silent clouds, and it was comforting to close the door upon approaching winter.

✻ ✻ ✻ ✻ ✻

In the few short, carefree months left before I started school, I grew very close to Mr Ford. I would follow him around the large garden, and he would teach me to, "Spake proper, like." Sometimes I sat high on a grass-filled wheelbarrow as he wheeled it to the compost heap in a far corner of the garden. Here grew fruit trees, shrubs and long, swaying grasses; a place of green shadow and ethereal whisperings. The swamp, sinister and brooding, would swell suddenly, quiver and emit a subterranean belch. Its breath smelt sweetly odorous. An amorphous cloud of mosquitoes hovered over it in green-filtered sunlight.

Great marrows grew at its edge. I would cower behind Mr Ford as he fed grass to this maleficent being, fearful yet awed.

* * * * *

One day Mr Ford appeared, beaming, at the lodge door. "Yur, missus, 'ave ee zeen the bay?"

Mum peered suspiciously from behind the half-open door as I emerged sheepishly from behind him. She shrieked and flung the door wide. "What on earth have you done to him?"

"Me, missus, I 'aven't done nort," Mr Ford chortled.

"Ee 'aven't done nort," I said.

"Vound un een the coal shed, I did, tryin' to climb the coal pile."

"Climbin' the coal pile, I wuz," I confirmed.

"Come in here!" Mum reached roughly around Mr Ford, knocking him aside and hauling me over the threshold. I was shocked; I'd never known her to be so rough. I started to cry.

"Why did you allow him to do it? You stupid man!" Mum was in full furious flow now.

"I just vound -" The door slammed in his face.

Later, Dad just grinned when Mum told him. And Mum sighed. Then grinned too.

* * * * *

Some weeks later, Dad said, "Those kittens, Madam's afraid of them turning feral, like their mother. She wonders if we would adopt one."

And so Puss entered our lives, a tabby kitten, playful and friendly. As she grew, she took to following us the length of the long drive, like a dog. Mum in a summer's dress and a floppy hat pushing my sister in her pram, me at her side and Puss beside us, sauntering, scenting the air, tiger-striped tail slightly crooked, cocked high. She would patiently await our return at the end of the drive, on a sun-warmed bank where dog roses fluttered like pink-tainted rice paper, their fragrance tantalizing in the flushed air.

RIVER MONSTER

"I'm taking the old cha salmon fishing," announced Mr Leslie, who was home on leave from the navy, tall, bluff, and jolly. "Teach him how."

And Dad beamed and looked jolly, too.

I tugged nervously at his sleeve. "Can I come, Dad, please, fishing?"

"Well, I ..."

Mr Leslie, tall and blonde, seemed to notice me for the first time. I felt very small. "If he wants," he said. "Must keep back, though; don't want a fly catching in the arse of his trousers."

Arse! He'd said arse! I looked at Mr Leslie with increased interest.

Dad laughed a little too loudly.

I was glad it wasn't me who'd said arse.

* * * * *

Now I entered the valley for the first time, descending a flight of rough-hewn steps through a rockery behind Dad and Mr Leslie. It seemed a long way down. Finally, we passed through a wooden gate into a field. The grass appeared much wilder from this level, coarse and hummocky, and I could hear the valley breathing; great breaths inhaled throughout the surrounding trees and accompanied by an ambient rushing sound. Both men wore satchels over their shoulders, thigh-high waders, and carried rods that whipped and snapped in the air as they walked. I trotted behind, pulling my socks high to avoid needle-sharp thistles.

I could hear the river clearer now, the rushing sound mutating into a shushing and rippling, and I realised it was the song of the river accompanied by a questing wind in the conifers rising steeply from the opposite bank. A ribbon of daffodils nodded cheerfully at me as I passed through their ranks and half-stumbled down onto a pebble beach where the river leaped and spun over shallows, spindrifts of foam like whipped cream. The pebbles clacked sharply as I crossed them, becoming suddenly insubstantial as they submerged at the water's edge. Dad and Mr Leslie were a few feet away, gazing down at something, and I walked towards them to see a huge silver fish dulled in death. Exposed bone glistened amidst tattered pink flesh in a jagged hole torn from the back of its head, around which buzzed excited, bejewelled blowflies. Tiny serrated teeth lined its gaping mouth. A waft of putrefaction assailed me and, nauseous, I backed a step.

"Bloody otters," said Mr Leslie.

Bloody! He'd said bloody! I looked nervously at Dad, who remained po-faced. "Still, can't blame them, I suppose," Mr Leslie continued, "it's their food after all. Hunt'll be along soon, anyway." He moved away to set up his rod and line.

An otter. What savage beast must that be? And to be hunted! I approached the river's edge warily, preparing to flee should the otter rise, a fanged and fearful monster, to reclaim its meal.

* * * * *

"I'm starting skewel t'morra," I informed Mr Ford.

"Aye, you'll be alright, then," said Mr Ford.

"Doris is taking me."

"Aye, you'm lookin' voorward to it, I reckon," Mr Ford said.

But I wasn't too sure of that. On the whole I'd rather stay with Mr Ford, rather follow Puss around, explore the copse across the drive to catch a half-glimpse of some shy creature amidst the swaying branches which sounded like the sea, baulk at some amorphous shadow-beast slinking between the trees, gaze in wonder at a patch of blue above the leafy canopy where buzzards circled lazily, their mewling cry descending to earth like falling sorrows.

* * * * *

So did the halcyon days of that first spring pass, until it was time for me to start school, where I was to discover new friends, other interests. Soon Mr Ford drifted into the background of my life, a diminishing shadow. Our two lives had dovetailed the centuries in a flawless join until one day, without my really noticing, he was gone.

* * * * *

"You ought to pick some flowers for Mr Ford's grave," Dad said on the anniversary of his death. "He was fond of you, you know."

So I picked some primroses and gave them a fern backdrop and placed them on his grave in the chapel cemetery high on the knoll and across from his cottage. But memory of him was already fading in my busy young life.

SCHOOL

Mum wanted to escort me all the way on my first day, but Dad said no. "Doris'll take him, he'll be perfectly alright, no need you trudging all the way there and back. Don't want to make a sissy of him."

So Mum escorted me across the fields to where Doris lived in one of the two farm cottages. There were cows in the fields and Mum was uneasy, skirting along the hedgerow while nervously eyeing the peacefully grazing bovines.

"Keep hold of my hand, duck," she said anxiously, and was relieved when we passed through a gate into the next field – until she felt the earth shudder under her feet and heard a loud, staccato snort as old Tom, the Shire horse, bore down upon us. Not hitched up to cart or plough today, he had been grazing tranquilly until we appeared, when he thought he'd investigate the two strangers.

Mum squeezed my hand tight and backed towards the gate. "It's alright, duck." Her voice quavered. "He won't hurt us."

Old Tom slowed, stopped a few feet from us. His great head nodded, his lips quivered, and steam came from his nostrils. He stamped one huge forefoot and the earth trembled again.

We gazed at each other.

Then Tom lowered his head and continued grazing.

After a while, Mum said softly, "I think it's alright duck, I think he's lost interest in us." And keeping close to the hedge we moved tentatively forward.

Old Tom raised his head and began to follow us.

Mum quickened her pace. "Just ignore him, duck. Don't look behind, duck, and he might go away." Mum's eyes swivelled. "He's like the milkman's horse really – just a bit bigger."

The milkman to me was but a distant memory; here, Dad always collected our milk from the farm early in the morning.

Kerlick, kerplunk, resounded Tom's hooves, pruuup, he snorted. A kind of friendly sound, I thought.

Even so, Mum seemed relieved when we reached the orchard gate. Inside, the apple trees were ancient, some fallen, others upright, some in between, all gnarled and battered by decades of the elements. A delicate froth of pink-tinted apple blossom billowed, casting a subtle fragrance over us.

I glanced behind us. Old Tom's head hung over the top bar of the gate. Pruuump! Steam jetted from his nostrils.

"There's a bull in the orchard, mind," Dad had told us. "He's tethered, of course," he said, adding, "usually."

Now Mum peered nervously into the orchard. Clasping my hand, she set off between the trees. One particular tree spread blossomed boughs wide over an area of churned earth. Coarse hairs were embedded in its trunk and it emitted a pungent bovine smell. Mum stared at it suspiciously and tightened her grip on my hand.

We glimpsed willow-brown cob outhouses through the trees, a gate leading into a farmyard... and there he was, in his rickety old lean-to backing onto the shippen wall; a huge, muscular beast with a vast head and down-turned horns. His dark, brooding eyes regarded us from the shadows with a kind of sad sagacity, his cumbersome form swayed lightly from side to side. He and I gazed with benign curiosity at each other.

"It's alright," said Mum. "He's chained up, he can't reach us."

And we passed through the gate.

* * * * *

As we crossed the rutted, earthen farmyard, ducks waddled lazily from our path, beady-eyed chickens pecked invisible delicacies from the stony ground. Tangled old sheepdog Ruff came bounding towards us. He knew us from previous visits and his tail thrashed welcomingly. He followed us as far as the cart shed where the lane led up to the cottages, gazed awhile, then ambled back.

Doris and her mum were waiting at the cottage door. The two mums greeted each other. Mrs Friend, plump and bosomy, was enveloped in a floral apron, her face shining and with a large wart rampant on the tip of her nose.

Doris smiled, a sweet-little-girl smile which didn't quite reach her eyes and elicited a tingle of unease within me. She was four years older than me, taller, too, with dark hair framing a chubby face.

"Doris'll look after un," Mrs Friend assured Mum. "No need to worry 'bout that."

* * * * *

And so off we set, along the lane, Doris holding my one hand, the other clasping my satchel. At the bend in the lane, I disengaged Doris's hand and turned to wave goodbye to Mum, an alarming lump forming in my throat. Mum waved back. She looked sad through her smile. For the first time we were separated.

* * * * *

I reached again for Doris's hand, but it wasn't there, neither was her smile.

"Don't think you c'n hang on to me all the time," she said. "You bain't a sissy, be ee?"

And thus began life's education away from Mum.

"Yur's Stacy," said Doris, nodding at a slight, nervous looking boy who materialised from a gateway. He wore a too-large cap which rested upon jug ears. He smiled hesitantly, exposing large teeth.

"Take thiky stupid grin off'n yer face," demanded Doris. "This's Boxall." She reached behind my head and pushed my cap over my eyes. "Ee's as daft as you be, I reckon."

And we trudged in silence away, my heart sinking. The lane was narrow and stony, and I stumbled once in a while.

"Oh, dear, whoops!" sneered Doris.

Every few feet a gap appeared in the hedge and I could see an orchard dropping steeply to the edge of a forest. The apple trees here, too, were gnarled and old, many fallen but still fruitful. Chickens foraged between and around them, talons kicking up little puffs of dust.

"Tell un 'bout old Mother Burton," she ordered Stacy.

Stacy's smile faded.

"Go on, tell un," she insisted irritably.

"Er's the taicher," Stacy informed me.

"Stupid bugger!" Doris aimed a slap at Stacy, which he ducked to avoid. "Course er's the taicher; tell un what er's like."

"Er's ... er's a bugger!" exclaimed Stacy. He grinned at his vocal extravagance.

"Er is, an' er'll soon sort un out, tell un that."

"Er'll soon sort ee out, sure nuff," Stacy told me.

"Big stick, er've got," continued Doris. "Catches ee right yur." She showed me the base of her thumb. "Right where it 'urts. Course, er only 'its the bays, not the maids. Maids don't git 'it. Er'll soon sort you out, sure nuff."

Another gap in the hedge and I saw a chicken shed, dark-creosoted, canting, some planks loose. On its apex perched a rooster, proud, feathers reflecting the sun like liquid gemstones. Its beady eyes eyed us balefully.

"Tell un 'bout thiky cock'ril," Doris demanded of Stacy.

"Oh, aye … ee 'ides, jumps out at ee, pecks'n chases ee."

"Ee does'n all; waits een one've they gaps … the side you'm on," exclaimed Doris.

My chest tightened.

I remained fearful until a sharp bend in the lane took us away from the hedge, tangled woodland now dropping away on one side, a high bank rising on the other.

"Spect ee'll get ee on the way 'ome," said Doris. "Ee know what time us comes along."

* * * * *

At the end of the lane a narrow country road banked by high hedges dropped down, past a hollow ash, and into Dolton Valley where, in tumbled cottages, lived Archie Parkhouse the trapper, Peg-leg Bob Brown, and the reclusive Phillips brothers, before rising in a long and winding climb to the village.

* * * * *

The school lay in the shadow of the village church, was built of granite blocks and with high windows which swung vertically open at 45 degrees on summer days at the pull of a bobbed cord. The cobbled playground was enclosed by a high wall over which bees swarmed on hot days ("The bees be swarmin', get eenzide, get eenzide!") and the tantalising scent of garden flowers drifted, but the sights of which were forever hidden from us.

* * * * *

On that first day Doris escorted me through a conflux of rowdy children to meet Mrs Burton. My heart was in my mouth, my eyes swivelling for a glimpse of the big stick, as Doris, beatific smile now back, introduced me to a stout, elderly white-haired lady who, I discovered over the coming months, was marking time until she could retire to her native Sussex. Or, as she informed us more than once, live in a flat overlooking Piccadilly, away from the languorous lazy drone of a rustic village, of sheep and cows and undulating farmland. Her husband was missing somewhere in Europe; only later did she discover he was a POW in Germany. And only later, too, did I discover that she really could whack you painfully on the base of your thumb!

Owing to a substantial influx of evacuees from London, the infants' class was temporarily in the village hall. The teacher, Miss Locke, was a slender young woman in her twenties with a tumble of golden hair, who told us the cat-sat-on-the-mat, that two and two make four, and most exciting of all, introduced us to Uncle Remus, Brer Rabbit and Brer Fox.

Across the road from the village hall, and concealed from the hoi polloi by iron railings and a privet hedge, was Miss Wadling's private school, patronized by children of landowners and the richer of the farmers. One of these children was Rachel, a farmer's daughter a couple or so years older than me. Spotting me outside the village hall one dinnertime, she, for reasons best known to herself, took a fancy to me and took me under her wing as if I were a younger brother. To this day I am haunted by the memory of my craven betrayal of her kindness, of which more later.

* * * * *

On the way home the cockerel was waiting. I glanced apprehensively at the canting chicken shed, but he was no longer there.

I eased surreptitiously back a step from Doris's side, began to shuffle behind her to Stacy's side.

"What do ee think you'm 'bout o'?" Doris swung around and hauled me back. "Oh! I see, you'm frightened of thiky there cockerel, be ee," she exclaimed, feigning sudden comprehension. "Well, ee've 'ad us, best you get a taste of un."

My heartbeat increased dramatically.

"Or best ee gets a taste've you, eh?" she smirked, nudging Stacy, who giggled timidly.

And in the first gap, there he was! Just his head visible, the garish plumage of his neck glinting amorphously, his ridged strawberry comb quivering. His eyes demon-fierce with malice.

"Run!" screamed Doris, and she and Stacy charged off down the lane.

Whimpering with terror, I followed, satchel flapping, legs flailing.

The cockerel charged as I passed the gap, a prism of gaudy fury. I felt the wind of his wings, heard his high-pitched war-cry and, crying shamelessly now, fuelled by blind panic and with the devil-bird's talons raking down my trousers, hurtled on down the lane to where Doris and Stacy stood waiting, grinning delightedly. I slammed into Doris, who thrust me roughly away. "Told ee, didn't I? Made ee cry, didn' un? Cry-baby," she said, as I hid behind her.

Peering back up the lane I saw him, cock-of-the-walk, head high, cackling in victorious splendour on the border of his domain.

By the time we reached the farmyard I was feeling ashamed. Here we parted ways. Stopping at the duck pond, I unbuttoned my fly. At the other side of the pond, peering through the hawthorn shrubs, I could see Doris and Stacy laughing heartily as I released an energetic stream into the murky water.

Mum was waiting at the orchard gate. She smiled broadly and took my hand. "Hello, duck. How did your first day go?"

* * * * *

I was in love with Hazel Martin. She was a good ten years older than me and played the piano for singing lessons. She had rich auburn hair, which gleamed like burnished oak in shafts of sunlight streaming through the window and tumbled in dappled splendour over her shoulders. Her face was of an exquisite and flawless beauty, and her long slender fingers danced dazzlingly across the keys. Her lips looked as soft and tender as rose petals. They puckered slightly as we sang *Sweet Lass of Richmond Hill*, and *Annie Laurie*. Her luminous green eyes moistened when we sang the lullaby, "Soft and Low Over, the Western Se-ea … Sleep my little one …"

As her arms undulated over the keyboard, I would catch a glimpse of the rise and fall of her breasts beneath the cotton blouse and experience a liquid sensation in my stomach. I imagined a fire: as others clambered to escape, I would dash to her rescue, sweep her weightlessly into my arms, smell the fragrance of her against me as I bore her to safety. She would turn in my arms and kiss me, her saviour.

But somewhere between the infants' and juniors', she faded opalescently away. What became of her? Did she marry a prince? No matter, because forever she will be my eternal beauty with burnished hair, enchanted green eyes, and haunting face.

THE MOVE

The Duttons were moving from the big house, not far, about two miles as the crow flies, three by road, where they had leased the 'Old Rectory', part of a manored estate. We moved from the lodge to one of the two farm cottages, next door to Doris.

Mum was beginning to look strained, resignedly weary, feeling she was being drawn inexorably deeper and deeper into a past age; an age before electricity, before plumbing and before Mr Crapper invented the water closet. For that was the way we now lived. At the Lodge we had shared a generator with the big house, but here we had oil lamps. Sometimes, recalling it, it seemed cosy and comforting, but I doubt Mum found it so. She did have a Calor gas cooker, at least.

There was a well at the bottom of a long garden, where newts, frogs and toads thrived, and from which Mum drew buckets of water for all our usage, queasily flicking out any captured amphibians. All laundry was done in a wood-fuelled boiler the size and shape of a witch's cauldron. On washing days (we had them then), Mum would toil up the garden path between vegetables and the chicken run, hauling two buckets of water, returning for another two, and so on, until the boiler was full.

Once, I fell into this well. It had a creaky, in-sloping wooden door. For some long-forgotten reason, I had hurtled full pelt down the path, palms spread to halt myself against this door, which instantly disintegrated on impact. Headfirst I went, down into the murky green depths, somehow turned turtle at the bottom, surfacing like a manic water-baby, grasping the well's rim, and shaking water from my eyes, "Da-ad!"

Dad, who was working in the garden, ran to my aid. "How on earth…?" And I was marched back to the house dripping silt, shivering and penitent.

* * * * *

Doris was approaching her teens now, and I began to see her through different eyes. I would take to lingering outside after dark, ostensibly looking for glow-worms, observing the bats, while my true intent was to lurk in the garden and surreptitiously peer up at Doris's bedroom window, hoping to catch her in the act of undressing. Sometimes I would see her shadow, flickering and infracted in the lamplight, glimpse her briefly, fully clothed. But as my bedtime was well before hers, this proved frustratingly unsuccessful.

I began to plot, considering burrowing a peephole behind a hanging picture on the dividing wall. But as the wall consisted of 24 inches of solid cob, this too, to say the least, was impractical. Thus, my nascent licentiousness was confounded.

However, Doris had not yet entirely outgrown her propensity for malicious mischief. She would hurl large stones onto the galvanized roof of our outside toilet from our adjoining gardens when she knew I was in there. The whole structure would reverberate, making me leap, trousers dangling around my ankles.

When I tentatively confronted her, "They there stones you 'eave is bending the galvanize," she would gaze at me with guileless innocence. "I dunno what you'm talkin' 'bout," she'd say.

INTIMATIONS OF WAR

The Dolton evacuees were all 'Lunnoners'. They and the local children eyed each other with mutual suspicion and more than a hint of contempt. On the Lunnoners' part, the local children were all backward yokels who spoke with a silly accent, had never visited a cinema or theatre and were utterly ignorant of street life; on the local children's part the Lunnoners were backward townees who spoke with a silly accent, had never seen a thrasher or binder, and didn't know milk came from cows nor eggs from chickens.

I, by this time, thanks to Mr Ford's tuition, spoke in a genuine rustic accent and had assimilated a rustic ethos, thereby aligning myself fully with the locals.

Gradually the two sides, to a certain extent, harmonised, as many of the Lunnoners, billeted on farms or with farm labourers' families, began to absorb the routine of country life. Football, too, was a great leveller, as was sex, even at those tender years.

One particular evacuee, a brash and sassy blonde from London's East End, precocious for her ten or so years, attracted boys of both groups like bees to honey. She would allow herself, with only token protest, to be manoeuvred into the coke shed by the older boys, where she would allow them a glimpse up the leg of her knickers. Excitement grew rapidly, along with nascent lust, and soon she was sprawled across the coke pile with her knickers around her ankles, and now protesting strongly. At this stage the boys would guiltily disperse, leaving her to readjust her clothing before emerging coke-smeared but strangely smug.

* * * * *

Then one day, like migrating birds, they were gone, back to Lunnon, and we infants moved back into the school, leaving the village hall to the Women's Institute and the Home Guard.

* * * * *

Often, convoys of troops – lorries, armoured cars, gun carriages – grumbled frighteningly along the narrow country roads, disturbing livestock, dogs, and locals alike, but never stopping.

Once, on my way to Sunday school, alone for some forgotten reason, I was a few yards up the road from the end of our lane when the birds fell silent. Just a whisper of breeze in the hedgerow... And then that growl like distant thunder, increasing, approaching... A trickle of ice in my stomach.

I turned abruptly, panic-stricken, began to run back to the lane.

Too late.

A covered army lorry, camouflaged, filling the narrow road never built for such things, clipping the hedge on either side. I leaped into the hedge, clawing as high as I could, hanging desperately onto a low ash bough. I began to whimper. The lorry rumbled past with a couple of feet to spare, the grass hissed. Its back was open, and lines of soldiers sat inside, staring blankly.

The convoy seemed endless: lorries, gun carriages which jerked and rumbled sinisterly, each vehicle a few feet behind the other. I scrabbled higher, sobbing freely now, seeing no sympathy on the soldiers' faces for the mewling wretch embedded in the hedge.

A break. The final lorry disappeared around the corner. I could hear it thunder across the bridge below, fade away on the far side.

I ceased sobbing, listened. A solitary blackbird chirped. Fearfully, I began to lower myself from the hedge. The blackbird flittered across the road, shrilling a warning. And again I heard it, that baleful growl, coming closer.

I whimpered, yelped, dropped onto the road, and ran helter-skelter for the end of the lane. I could hear it nearing fast, a continuous growl.

But I had made it!

I was suddenly fearful of what Dad would say. Should I have somehow carried on to Sunday school? Was I a cissy?

In the event, Dad just grinned and said it was okay, not to worry.

Such a relief to be home and safe.

✵ ✵ ✵ ✵ ✵

"The Yanks be comin' and they'm gonna stop!" went up the cry, and a shimmer of anticipation rippled through the village.

We children sat through our morning lessons with barely concealed excitement.

"You know what you've gotta zay to 'em."

"What? What do ee zay?"

"You gotta zay, 'Ave ee got any gum, chum?'"

"An' they'll give it to ee?"

"Yea, I reckon."

"Git away wi' ee!"

"Yeah, tis true, sure nuff, I've yurd it on the wireless."

* * * * *

They arrived during our dinner hour. Roared into the village square, gravel crunching and spurting under their wheels as they swung in. We watched in awe as they descended from the backs of lorries, vaulted from jeeps, milled around, eyed us suspiciously.

We stayed silent awhile, fascinated by the rolling twang of accents we'd only ever heard on the wireless: Phil Harris, Tennessee Ernie Ford, Bob Hope and Bing Crosby. Cowboys!

Faces peered from behind curtains in cottage windows; villagers strode slowly past, staring openly.

"Go on, ask 'em."

"You ask 'em."

"No, you."

Farmer John's old collie-dog trotted past with a quiet dignity, a basket of groceries from the village store clasped proprietorially in his jaws, oblivious to all the excitement.

"Gee, lookie at that dawg, he's gone done the goddarn shopping!"

"Well, my!"

"He's jis like ma gran's ol' Rover."

They chuckled good humouredly, clasping pints of beer purchased from the Royal Oak across the square.

"Go on then, ask 'em."

"You, you ask 'em."

Eventually, one of the bolder boys sidled hesitantly up to a lorry, gazed at the soldiers lounging there. They gazed back, unsure of this alien urchin.

"Got any gum, chum?"

They continued to stare.

"Sure kid, here." Packets of chewing gum were tossed to us, and we scrambled unashamedly for them. "Now scat!"

We scat.

Soon they were gone – gravel flying, gears meshing, engines roaring, a haze of petrol fumes and blue-grey smoke rising in their wake – possibly, for many of them, to their deaths in the D-Day landings.

When they stopped in our village, how it was known in advance that they would, I never asked, didn't know and never will now.

✳ ✳ ✳ ✳ ✳

Our lavatory, rather a grand title for a 4 x 4 wooden shack boasting a round-holed plank with a galvanized bucket beneath, lay across the lane in the shade of a beech tree rooted in the Friend's garden. When full, Dad would cart the bucket past the Friend's front door to empty it in a far corner of our garden.

One summer's day, Land Girls arrived, gay and laughing, jesting and singing in the back of a covered lorry, and vaulted out to enter the field bordering the Friend's garden and our toilet. They gathered in the stooked corn under a torrid sun, tossing it from the cart to Mr Friend who, rising gradually higher, corn-dust slathered by sweat to his forehead, expertly ricked it.

However, the girls, seeming not conversant enough with country ways to disappear behind a hedge when necessary, used our toilet.

Dad was now cycling daily the three miles to the Old Rectory and back. The girls had already departed, chattering and weary and sheathed in wheat dust, before he arrived home, where he raged and seethed as he emptied the overflowing bucket before swabbing out the shack.

* * * * *

It was not always Land Girls. Before them it was Italian POWs. I would stand fascinated, watching them disembark from the lorry, dark eyes flashing, swarthy skins and mops of bouncing black hair, and all looking so cheerful, chattering incomprehensibly in a strange language, exotic and wonderful to my young ears. Some of them would flash me a smile, their teeth gleaming, and say something to me in that lilting voice, and I wondered how they could possibly be bad men, our enemies.

They had a different sort of smile for Doris. They would gesture and laugh, and their eyebrows would rise and fall, and Doris would go all bashful in a way I'd never seen her do before, scuttling off indoors only to furtively reappear in a corner of her window a few moments later.

They would decamp into the fields, still chattering animatedly, to pick up potatoes, turn the hay or stook the corn, depending on the season.

Then one day they were gone, and it was the Land Girls. I don't know, but I guess it was after their compatriots slaughtered their leader and his mistress and strung them upside-down from a street lamppost, then changed sides.

* * * * *

It was faint at first, a distant hum, ululating slightly like a summer song. No one took much notice. It increased, grew louder, the song took on a threatening note. Birds in hedgerows fell quiet, Puss ran indoors, and our chickens sauntered unsure into their coop.

It was coming closer, a phantasma of sound, guttural now, aggressive. Puss slunk under my bed upstairs.

Mrs Friend and Doris appeared at their back door and Mum joined them from ours, flanked by my sister and me.

"What on earth be it?" wondered Mrs Friend, in a hushed voice.

"I dunno," said Mum.

They fell silent, gazing into the lowering sky, the sound-wall all around now, all encompassing, rolling gratingly.

"Look!" Doris pointed beyond the ancient beech tree where the field met the sky.

We couldn't make them out at first, like pterodactyls breaking through a time warp.

"Goodness!" said Mum.

"Well my," said Mrs Friend. "Will ee look't that!"

49

The sky was thick with them, coming at us from below a sullen cloud blanket, seeming to skim the field.

"Tis airplanes," exclaimed Mrs Friend.

"No tidn't," said Doris.

"Course tis," said her mother.

"They're towing something," said Mum.

"Oh, my!" exclaimed Mrs Friend. "Tis they there glider thangs, they'm towing gliders."

And they were. The sky was thick with them now, like nightmare locusts. Their guttural drone filled the air, shivered the grass, echoed sluggishly around our houses and sheds, throbbed in the old beech, setting its leaves atremble. They came in waves, slowly, methodically. We gazed, amazed and silent, heads turned to the sky in awed wonder.

Then they were gone, trailing their funereal war-song behind them, across the river and over the trees into hell.

* * * * *

It was a Friday evening, a stay-up night for me and my sister Valerie. No school tomorrow. It was late autumn, there was a chill in the air and the nights were drawing in. We were all indoors, listening to *Happidrome* ("Eh, Mr Luuvejoy!" "What is it,

Enoch?") or maybe it was *Merry-Go-Round* ("A large one? Ah, don't mind if I do sah!") on the wireless.

Warmth flowed from the large open fireplace, the great backlog glowing and flickering ruby-red, logs crackling soothingly. Puss stretched contentedly before it with me seated on a stool beside her. Night pressed against the windowpanes and I imagined the nocturnal creatures in the woods, which I never saw but only sensed on my daytime forays, would have emerged, padding their secret trails, the woods theirs now. And maybe some larger creatures too: shadowy and predatory. Either way, it was nice to be safe indoors.

Suddenly the whole house juddered, windowpanes rattled, shaking awake the torpid night, the oil lamp jiggled across the table, its flame leaping alarmingly. At the same time came a frightening rumble of thunder, except it wasn't thunder: too muffled, too terrestrial.

Mum and Dad looked at each other. The musty-dank smell of air-raid shelter, near-forgotten, skittered like a needle-legged spider through me.

The Friend family were already outside their back door, where Mum and Dad joined them. My sister and I remained inside in the warm pool of friendly lamplight. We gazed at the backs of the adults. Darkness slithered around them to sneak cold fingers indoors.

"'Tiz a bomb fer zure!" we heard Mr Friend say. He sounded excited.

"There, look," said Dad.

Over his shoulder I could see a maleficent glow pulsating grotesquely in the shattered night.

"Oh, my!" exclaimed Mrs Friend.

"Like back home," said Dad, in the feigned nonchalance of we've-seen-it-all-before.

"Where's it to, you reckon?" asked Mrs Friend.

There was a pause as they considered the local topography.

"'Tis well down-stream," mused Mr Friend. "Below Ashcroft there 'bouts, I'd say."

"What hon earth be thur fer 'em t'bomb thur?" puzzled Mrs Friend.

No-one had an answer to this, so they stayed a while talking, their voices acute in the night air, until the malignant glow lessened, then, "Night," said Dad.

"Night each," chorused Mr and Mrs Friend cheerily.

And each returned indoors, partly excited, partly disturbed that the violence of war was real and had briefly touched them.

Next day a large phalanx of villagers trudged intrigued and anticipatorily down West Lane and along the riverside path, crossing fields and skirting bogs, through copses, to below Ashcroft where a yawning crater gaped, surrounded by fallen, splintered trees and several dead sheep; birds too, blasted from their roosts by man's destructive taste for violence.

"Would ee look't that!"

"Oh, my!"

"What hiver be it comin' to!"

"Twas a bomb, zure nuff."

"What did 'em drop un yur vur, then, you reckon?"

"Dumpin' thur remainin' load, I yurd, comin' back vrum a Plymouth Docks raid."

"Aye, most like."

"Buggers they be they Jerries, 'n' no mistake!"

"Varmer Baker's lost a vu shape there, that's vur sure."

"Lucky twadn' ee! Ee's varm's jist up thur."

"Rooks've been at 'em already, looks like, 'n' magpies."

"Ee'll zell 'em, I reckon. Butcher Vishleigh'll be glad've 'em."

"Ee'll 'ave t'declare 'em t'government, I reckon, mait bein' on ration an' all."

"Wot, like ee daid ee's paig, then!"

Laughter.

"Less said 'bout that the better."

Laughter, a brief pause, a faint whiff of roast mutton.

"Git out, tis a maisterpaice, you, zure nuff."

* * * * *

Today the bomb crater is a large pond sequestered by nature, alive with newts, frogs and toads amidst reeds and bulrushes; damselfly and dragonfly larvae flourish there, squiggly creatures wriggle in its muddy depths. Trees surround it protectively, casting green-dappled shade. It lies now in a nature reserve, tranquil and beautiful.

Few people are aware of its genesis.

* * * * *

The rest of the war never touched us directly; the occasional sinister glow in the night sky over Plymouth fifty miles distant, or thirty-odd miles to the east over Exeter; Land Girls; the ominous wavering drone of an aeroplane; rationing. But school went on as normal, the farming cycle of tilling and harvests, the clock put back two hours in summer, staying light until eleven at night, when the workers would trundle wearily to their lamplit cottages, dusty, sweaty, and hungry and cursing the torturous barley ails in their socks and underwear.

SHEEP

They flowed around a bend in the lane like a tarnished foam of floodwater, bleating energetically under a shimmering swarm of midges and the aroma of fresh mutton. Ruff flitted swift and stealthy as a panther, herding them along.

Our chicken coop lay on a patch of grassy wasteland between the lane and our cottage and Mum, having just fed the hens, was gathering eggs from the nest boxes, Valerie and I hovering somewhat bored behind her, when we all paused to gaze at the heaving flock. Golden eyes glinted under the sun, dust rose, turd-currants tumbled and rolled; dead brambles were tangled in the wool of some of the ewes like implements of medieval torture.

Suddenly a sheep detached itself from the flock like wind-blown spume, no ewe this, but large and muscular with lowered head and horns like rock-hewn fossils, testicles swaying like raw doughboys. It came straight at us, silent and lethal. Mum screamed, grabbed Valerie, and slung her like a sack of potatoes onto the top of the coop's wire enclosure, then scrambled up behind her, skirt billowing, stockings snagging, one shoe falling off as she yelled at me to do the same; a needless behest, as I was already on.

The ram's head slammed into the chicken run, which twanged and hummed like a shattered piano. The hens inside squawked and cackled hysterically, milling around in numb panic as the ferocious beast razed the wire, with its horns creating a demented fugue, before Ruff appeared to herd it back to the flock, leaving Mum and we two children crouching atop an ominously sagging chicken-wire roof. One of the wooden holding-slats snapped like a gunshot as we jerked lower.

"Quick, duck, get off, it's breaking!" Mum, skirt snagged high, both stockings laddered, struggled desperately from the now concave wire, followed by a giggling pair of children.

"It's nothing to laugh at! It could've gored us, could've killed us," scolded Mum.

But by now Valerie and I were doubled up in rapturous delight at the sight of a bedraggled Mum, a red-faced mad-woman, skirt askew, stockings torn and wrinkled, slowly descending from the top of the coop. "Look at the chicken-wire, look at the wire!" we guffawed joyously. "What you gonna tell Dad?"

"What've ee been up to, missus? You look proper flushed."

Mum glanced up to see a grinning Mr Friend rounding the bend at the rear of the flock. "That blessed ram!" she cried. "Came right at us, could've killed us!"

"Yeah ..." Mr Friend removed his stained cap and scratched his head. "Ee's 'n' eller sure nuff, thiky."

"Could've killed us," insisted Mum.

"Oh, I doubt that, missus." Mr Friend gazed with amusement at the sagging chicken-wire. "You've made a bit've a dent een thiky, though," he grinned.

Further discourse was prevented by a lamb, its wool still a mass of cream-white curls and with the trusting face of the still-innocent and very young, dashing eagerly from the flock towards us. Its tail flailed and quivered as it brushed against our legs, bleating plaintively, moving from one to the other of us and gazing up questioningly. Valerie and I cooed and bent to fondle it as it eagerly sought our fingers to suck upon. Mum, ever the animal lover, smiled and baby-talked to it, our alleged brush with violent death temporarily forgotten.

"Ee was one've twins 'n' ee's mother rejected un," said Mr Friend. "So the maister's wife 'and-weaned un wi' a bottle."

We aahed in sympathy.

"Ee's old nuff now to rejoin the flock, though," added Mr Friend, picking the lamb up. "Come on, back us go, youngster." And he strode off after the flock, Ruff darting, swerving, rounding up any stragglers as we watched them disappear around the cottages like a soiled and flea-bitten cloud.

Mum gazed after them, still smiling. "Dear little thing," she said. "I hope he adapts alright to being a sheep."

We gazed at her.

"He *is* a sheep, Mum," I said.

FIREWORKS NIGHT

Fireworks night. Well-wrapped in coats, scarves, woollen gloves, we set off, two families – us and the Friends – over two stiles and through the winding lane to Dolton where there would be the communal bonfire and fireworks. It was a clear night with air cutting as a new razor blade and a velvet sky gilded with stars like burnished pearls. There was no moon that night, only the stars winking and gleaming, and I thought I'd never seen them so bright, so alive. I realised I could see others behind them which, if I looked really hard, seemed to move, coalesce in mother-of-pearl. Then I got giddy, stumbled, and almost fell.

Ahead of me, the others were veiled figures trailing star-shadow like rippling ghosts over the unploughed corn stubble.

"What be 'em, really, I wonder?" said Mrs Friend, gazing skyward.

"I don't know," said Mum. "Like holes in the sky letting light shine through."

"From Heaven," added Mrs Friend.

They pondered this in meditative silence as I caught up.

"Nah," decided Doris, "I reckon they'm a lot bigger 'n they look, though, cos they'm so high up."

"Why don't 'em fall down, then?" asked her mother.

"Cos they'm flat, of course! Float like snowflakes."

"Tiny sparkly little things, you could hold them in the palm of your hand," opined Mr Friend.

And I imagined one, ever so slightly tickly, soft, and friendly in my palm. I'd like that.

"Nay, they'm big," insisted Doris, loftily.

And I imagined one falling from the sky, a great, glowing sovereign pulsing cool and silent, spread across the field.

By now we had reached the last stile and clambered over, with much giggling and squealing from the women. Ahead, the lane tunnelled through overhanging trees and hedge-top shrubs, woodland closing in on either side and starlight now broken by a lacework of branches. Torches were turned on. We proceeded in single file, Dad leading. I had followed this lane to school every day, but now, night-time, it suddenly seemed sinister, dreamlike. Spectral figures, ghouls, and goblins crouched waiting to pounce from the hedgerows. Phantoms swooped down upon me, strange snicks and rustlings kept pace with us from within the woodland. Stalking wolves! I was last in file and something was creeping up behind me. I pressed close to Mum's side.

"Whoops! Careful, duck."

On her other side, Valerie peered knowingly, a mocking grin on her face. "Ee's scared of the dark," she said.

"Not!"

"Ghosties 'n' things."

"Shuddup! Daft ol' maid."

"You be."

"Bain't! Anyway, bain't no such things's ghosties."

* * * * *

We emerged from the lane into unbroken starlight, and down into the combe where we could hear the brook tinkling over its icy bed. The mysterious Romany caravan with its gaily painted sides showed faintly through the trees on our right with the lights of Rock Cottage glowing high above. The dogs started barking as we passed Archie's, fierce and snarly and you could just tell they were slavering over gleaming fangs. I hoped Archie had them secure.

Archie himself didn't appear.

"Already in the pub, I reckon," said Mr Friend.

"Will ee listen to they dogs!" said Mrs Friend, with a shudder.

And they were in a frenzy now, hearing us but unable to see or get at us. They were still at it when we reached the crossroads.

"Look at that!" exclaimed Mum, suddenly, pointing.

A luminous glow, a tiny fairy lamp low down in the hedge. But, deep in the hedgerow grass, it became dislodged and fell before extinguishing itself. Not a glow-worm, I thought, but a fallen star, soft and delicate and imbued with the magic of a winter's night.

✻ ✻ ✻ ✻ ✻

We left the frozen night, its silent stars, and frost-dusted fields, and entered Dolton village.

Retreating now, the stars shrank haughtily away from the lamp-lit cottages from which light spilled into the street, pushing back the darkness. Fireworks were already going off spasmodically and we could see tongues of red and yellow flickering spectrally across the street, even before we turned the corner into the village square.

Then, there it was, a vast bonfire in the centre of the square, crackling, shooting flames, popping sparks which spiralled angrily away to join the stars, its heat spreading to embrace us.

"Tis a masterpiece fer zure," said Mr Friend, as we all stopped to stare with shining eyes.

"Let's hope the wind doesn't spring up," said Dad, eyeing the surrounding thatched cottages.

Light from the flames danced and spun over the walls of the Royal Oak fronting the square. Drinkers stood outside, clasping pint glasses, laughing and chattering, their shadows sending animated demons to prance over the wall. Jackson's horse was absent tonight as were any dogs or cats, for this was a night of human unhallowedness and necromancy. Children jigged and flitted around the bonfire, their faces glowing red. Some carried turnip lanterns with jeering faces and rotten-stump teeth. Valerie and I rushed to join them, for Halloween had not yet got a grip in this country, was still an American thing; this was our English night to celebrate the hanging drawing and quartering of Captain Guy Fawkes, and maybe darker, more ancient rituals. Fawkes was atop the fire, flames licking at his straw-stuffed overall legs, a silly grin on his rag face below the greasy trilby.

I ran now with the other boys; Dennis, Trevor, Kenny Horrel and Dave Clements, Trevor Heard; shrieking with excitement, the latent genes of our distant pagan ancestors flickering temporarily awake. Someone had acquired squibs and these we threw at the feet of girls and women, making them squeal and rage in protest as we scuttled off, laughing cruelly at their crazy dancing. One of us recklessly threw a banger into the flames which exploded amidst a shower of sparks like enraged wasps.

"Aia! You little 'ellers, whathiver be ee 'bout o' … Come yur'n I'll box your blinkin' yurs!"

We ran down the back alleys we knew so well, touched by sorcery tonight, lamps glowing in the windows of quaint cottages, dancing prisms of light on frost-membraned garden shrubs. Pools of Stygian darkness lay under the eaves of antiquated barns, lurked in gaps between the weathered planks wherein witches and trolls lay await in ambush. We quickly averted our eyes and ran on, seeking further mischief. Down the narrow lane between looming stone walls we sauntered to where the sign of the Ram's Head hung over half beer-barrels containing dead flowers from a forgotten summer. Light from the windows, beer-scented warmth, laughter, and raucous male voices spilled onto the cobbled yard outside and we paused briefly, intrigued by this mysterious fraternity of grown men.

Back through the gate into the darkened alley bordering the war memorial, names of village war-dead we were too young to remember but whose ghosts would be poignantly hovering tonight, recalling such times of their own cut-short lives.

Two figures, entwined as one, turned their faces bashfully to the wall as we rushed past them, giggling, half-aware of what they were doing, nascent lust stirring within us.

"Did ee zee who twas?"

"Derick Marden'n some maid."

"Twadn'!"

"Twas!"

"Giddout!"

✻ ✻ ✻ ✻ ✻

Things were livening up in the square now. Fireworks were fizzing and exploding, Catherine wheels spinning. Men had emerged from the Royal Oak, others were making their way up from the Ram's

Head. Tongues of light quavered and undulated over them, and a shimmer of expectancy now pulsed through the night.

"They'm gwain fer old Mother Isaacs," one of us said.

A vague air of menace now hovered over the scene.

Some youths were already gathering in a small group at the top of the square, outside the house of Mrs Isaacs. Its door was closed, a faint light showed through the curtains. The house seemed to shrink into the shadows of its small front garden.

We sauntered up to stand behind the youths. A squib was thrown, skittered kittenishly into the garden.

An anticipatory pause.

Another squib, this time dancing along the windowsill. Now a banger, exploding; momentarily lighting up a laurel bush inside the garden gate.

There was no true malevolence in the intimidators, just a rather cruel sense of mischief. Had Mrs Isaacs restrained her indignation, remained indoors, we all would soon have drifted away to seek other distractions.

But she didn't; she fell for it every year. She was a woman with a sense of superiority; probably justified, as she was a well-spoken, articulate ex-teacher, lean and severe with a no-nonsense demeanour. She came charging out, voicing a tirade of contempt at we ignorant yokels, who only laughed and jeered and threw fireworks as she defiantly stood her ground. No husband had ever been seen, although there must once have been one, because she had an attractive daughter and a son, Tommy, with pudding-basin-cut black hair and a jerky, nervous manner, whom she nicknamed Dinky. Unwisely, she used to call him in when he played with us in the square. "Mummy wants you, Dinky," we would mimic. "Off you go, Dinky."

Both siblings remained sensibly indoors.

Not so their mother, who stood at her front gate emanating an aura of fearless scorn for we ill-educated bucolics, which only served to increase our derisive laughter.

"You're just a mob of pathetic rabble, I know who you are, you … you morons!"

"You know me then, do ee, missus?" cried a middle-aged farm labourer old enough to know better. He turned and lowered his corduroy breeches to moon a mottled and voluminous backside at her. "I'll show ee 'oo I be, missus!"

The crowd roared its delighted approval.

Mrs Isaacs, lost for further words, cast a look of pure disdain over all of us before sweeping regally back inside to a chorus of cheers, and slamming the door.

The show was over, and we all drifted back to the now declining bonfire, the drinkers back to the public bars of the two pubs.

"What do ee reckon to it, then, Bail?" someone asked Dad, grinning.

"Pretty poor show," declared Dad, firmly and with some commendable distaste.

And, deep in my heart, I was proud of him.

✳ ✳ ✳ ✳ ✳

The night sparkled like a legion of jewels; polished stars intense above, frost riming hedge, field and woodland, and the air biting our throats as we covered our mouths with scarves. Silence rang through the night, a time of magic when the world renewed itself as we slept. We were hushed, the adults quiet as we crossed the pathfield. Stars winked and sparkled like blue ice-shards overhead, and far below in the valley the river murmured in melodious solitude where the great shadow of Halsdon Wood rose to touch the glacial sky.

As we entered Brightley Cottage, we heard a skitter of movement, and in Dad's torch-beam an army of large black beetles scurried back to the warm open fireplace to vanish like magic between the stones. By the time Mum had lighted the oil lamp it was as if we had imagined them.

Tonight was one of those rare nights when Valerie and I were happy to go to bed.

GEORGIE

We named him Georgie. I don't know where we got him from. He was a gosling of foamy white with a yellow beak and startled beady eyes above a long slender neck. Valerie and I oohed and aahed delightedly, taking turns to gently hold and stroke him as he struggled ineffectively, his large orange-webbed feet padding softly against our palms, his delicate little head oscillating, no doubt anxiously seeking the lost security of his mother and siblings.

"Don't get too fond of him," Dad advised us, adding unambiguously, "he's our Christmas dinner."

"Ooh!" we said.

But on a scented spring morning of mayflower and bluebells and endless daylight, Christmas seemed yet a hundred years away, and we surrendered him to the care of a mother duck who had lost a couple of her own brood, Dad keeping an anxious eye less she reject him.

She did not, and that spring he considered himself a duck, happily cohabiting with his adoptive brood waddling in sinuous line behind the mother, slip-slapping joyously in warm mud, trailing through lengthening grass and nettles, red campion, and yellow rattle on a patch of wasteland across the lane, dabbling up ambiguous titbits in imitation of mother duck and quacking in gay communion with his siblings.

But as spring evolved into summer, fruit ripened and days were long and warm, Georgie grew, and grew fast. The mother and her ducklings began to look uneasy as he towered over them. He continued to grow, and their unease turned to alarm as Georgie, blithely unaware of his increasing size, padded close behind them. He began to shriek, a shrill and vibrant goose-shriek, and that did it. Mother and ducklings took off, lickety-split. Georgie, oblivious to their fear, split-splatted behind them. Down the path they went, around the plum tree and along the hedge, Georgie in close pursuit (Wait for me!)

After which he kept a wary distance. Meticulously preened and cleaned his soiled feathers. The days lessened, leaves lost their lustre, curled, and began to fall; apples, unpicked, fell to sustain wasps, blackbirds, and red admirals. A dampening mist began to rise from the river at dusk. Georgie grew fat. Substantially fat.

"Us bain't gwain to Dad, not really, be us?"

"That's what we got him for, and he's costing us in grain," Dad said. "He's not a pet, he's a goose. I told you, you mustn't get so attached," he reminded us.

Darkness now pursued us on the way home from school, almost catching us at the cottage door. A gale came and flayed the trees to skeletal bones and the river burst its banks, transforming the landscape to a turgid brown lake where once had been fields. And Georgie was shut in at night, cosy in his straw-lined hutch.

* * * * *

School broke up for the Christmas holidays.

"Be us really gwain to, Dad? Not poor Georgie!" we pleaded.

But the magic of approaching Christmas fevered our veins, and with the expedient resilience of children we accepted the inevitable.

Two days before Christmas, Mr Friend came, smiling, to lift a trusting Georgie and escort him away for execution (Dad baulking at the idea of perpetrating the deed himself). Valerie and I watched his plump white form bob away under Mr Friend's arm, his uncomprehending head turning gracefully atop his slender neck, blissfully unaware of his imminent fate.

Christmas Day: the intoxicating excitement of presents, family warmth, and the annual feast excluded all else from our minds, only eliciting the briefest pang of melancholy as Dad carved the Christmas goose.

I felt a twang of guilt at the first mouthful, but it tasted really good, much better than rabbit.

CHRISTMAS

Christmas was a magical interlude, just two days back then; Christmas Day and Boxing Day. For weeks before, Dad would lock himself in his shed after work and I would hear sawing and hammering and the hiss of the Tilley lamp as he secretly constructed toys for Valerie and me from any available materials, mainly wood. He was no carpenter and they were rough-hewn, but we were delighted, and cherished them. He would take one day off work the week prior to Christmas, when we would all cycle the couple of miles to the crossroads, leave our bikes in the hedgerow and catch the local bus to either Bideford or Okehampton. This was our annual trip to town, so a time of high excitement for myself and Valerie. We would gaze in wonder at all the people and the shops. Mum and Dad would occasionally distract our attention but we knew why, although we pretended not to, sneaking looks at some wondrous toy or book which we knew was destined for our Christmas pillowcases.

Whilst warmly wrapped and seated on a park bench or in some convenient shelter, we would eat sandwiches Mum had made before leaving home, drink tea from a flask, our dog Micky nudging our knees for titbits until ordered by Dad, "Sit!" Finally we would cycle home from the crossroads, under the stars and between frost-spangled hedgerows, with Mum and Dad laden and wobbling precariously and Micky lolloping behind.

Hours of daylight were short and severe, increasing darkness holding a promise of the approaching big day. My friend Trevor and I spent brief hours outdoors, doggedly traipsing the naked woods, the barren fields, seeking mysteries to solve. Enid Blyton children always seemed to find some. We found none, only a grey-green landscape bereft of concealment in skeletal woods, cold hands and feet, red running noses. Only Micky truly enjoyed these forays, tracking rabbits, scenting foxes and, seemingly immune to the cold, plunging recklessly into the icy river. Dusk came mid-afternoon and we were secretly glad to retire indoors.

"Zee ee tomorrow, then."

"Yeah."

"If tidn't rainin'."

"Yeah."

* * * * *

It was the season of bumper edition comics, which I devoured hungrily, lingering over margins portraying holly, snow, and Christmas puddings topped with brandy sauce and a red-berried holly sprig. It always snowed in comic Christmases, characters were jolly, dogs ran off with the Christmas turkey and Scrooges received their comeuppance.

* * * * *

"I need you to help saw the logs," Dad said.

Cold at first, I would soon get warm on my end of the crosscut-saw as the logs fell and sawdust flew like winter midges in the light of the faithful Tilley lantern as frost glistened and ice sparkled over the stony lane, and the night pressed in upon us. Micky sat at the edge of the light, happy merely to be with us. Pausing as a log fell, we could hear the murmur of the river in the valley below, the hoot of an owl somewhere across the fields as the moon appeared over the rim of the meadow.

* * * * *

On the evening of the Sunday school Christmas party we would trudge through the darkness to chapel, where the long trestle table groaned under a mouth-watering feast of egg and bacon pie, ham sandwiches, mince pies, junket, and Christmas cake marzipanned and iced and dotted with silver balls which could gouge out your tooth fillings if you weren't careful. We played musical chairs, and postman's knock, when I would secretly hope to get to kiss the exquisite raven-haired, cute-nosed, and dark-eyed Evelyn Squires, but usually ended up with Dennis's raw-faced mother – or Doris! We played hunt the sixpence, traditionally to be found hidden in aged Mr Chamming's kiss curl.

Finally, home, an icy wind rising, humming in the telephone wires above the amorphous hedgerows as a group of us chattered happily under a warm shield of amity.

✻ ✻ ✻ ✻ ✻

Christmas Eve, and we would pass the day impatient for evening: a ghost story on the wireless, flickering candlelight casting spidery shadows on the staircase on the way to bed, a pillowcase on the bedpost. I knew there was no Father Christmas – Stacy had told me – but I still wanted to believe, and in the crisp air of that enchanted night anything was possible. I thought I would never get to sleep; tossed and turned tingling with excitement. Then, without realizing it, I drifted off.

I awoke in the early hours, took a second to remember, then jolted awake. The pillowcase now bulged intoxicatingly, and I stared at it in wonder.

What time was it? No one was up yet. Waiting was torment. Eventually I heard Valerie awaken, heard her rush into Mum and Dad's room, the hiss and thump of a trailed pillowcase.

From that moment on the day was bathed in a warm glow of happiness, joy and love and family harmony; from the exquisite delving into our pillowcases for wondrous things, through Christmas dinner of goose with all the trimmings (a silent prayer for Georgie); the sun-drenched spirit of a summer's day manifested by runner beans Mum had salted down, followed by Christmas pudding containing a hidden treasure of silver threepenny bits. That day, plus Boxing Day, was isolated in a cocoon of warmth and magic and love, to be coveted down all the months until next Christmas.

REX

"Ee dud'n like it if ee thinks you'm fightin', you know," said Mrs Friend.

I'd been making a fuss of their dog Rex, a friendly light-haired collie-cross.

"You watch this yur," she said, laughing, a twinkle in her eye. "C'mon, Doris, come yur. I was tellin' Allan ... 'tend us be 'avin' a fight."

And they set to, giggling happily, twisting lightly with Mrs Friend's ample, matronly bosom bouncing alarmingly over Doris.

Rex's head jerked up. He shot away from me to leap between them, barking shrilly, separating them, then jumping from one to the other as they patted and fussed him. "Ee's a guid bay though, idn't un? Ee's a guid ol' lad."

Looking back, I wonder if he really thought they were fighting, or, more likely, just wanted to join in the game.

* * * * *

It was a humid day, hot, sticky. Birds temporarily ceased singing, perched silent in the shade of trees and hedgerows, plants wilted under the heat. Buzzards, little more than black dots on a vast canvas, glided high, lazily, on cooler currents.

Two sturdy Shire horses, Punch and Lion, gleamed with sweat as they stoically, uncomplainingly, pulled the corn binder under the reins of Mr Friend. The bladed teeth glittered shark-like under the sun, chattered manically, severing the tall wheat, and sending it rippling up the spread canvas to be swallowed, sheaved, and tied, then regurgitated ready to be stooked.

I would follow the binder, fascinated by the tide of golden wheat interspersed with delicate rose-pink pea-flowers, cornflowers of dusted blue, sapphire trumpets of field bindweed; not weeds to my seven-year old eyes, but nature's sparkling jewels. Corn-dust shaken from the ears of wheat rose and swirled in a saffron cloud, caressing the horses, Mr Friend and myself in a sun-blessed opalescence. Sometimes a tiny vole or field-mouse would scuttle sinuously away from the blades and I would hold my breath as it veered nimbly away through the stubble.

Families of pheasants or partridges emerged, squawking furiously, and Mr Friend briefly halted Lion and Punch, allowing the confused fawn-coloured half-grown chicks to dart hither and thither, zig-zagging away. The horses, steam rising from their flanks in smoky clouds, snorted dust from their nostrils and shook their heads, thankful for the momentary respite.

As the afternoon lengthened, a cheerful team of farm wives would appear with baskets of food – egg and bacon pie, cheese and pickles with home-baked bread, pasties, apple pie with lashings of yellow-crusted clotted cream – and the workers would squat in the shade of the binder or stooks of corn, wipe the engrained sweat from their brows and eat hungrily, chatting between draughts of cider and cold tea. Punch and Lion were fed ears of grain and chopped apples and were presented with buckets of cool water.

The sun, at its zenith, shot fiery arrows of heat, and handkerchiefs were draped under caps and over necks to prevent sunstroke, shirts were opened wide and sleeves rolled high as work recommenced.

The area of corn lessened as the binder doggedly circled it and the first rabbits, secure until now amidst the tall corn, began to bolt; they had been inexorably herded towards the centre of diminishing wheat, increasingly distant from their hedgerow warrens, until they finally panicked and broke cover. One or two unlucky ones headed directly into the slashing blades, their squeals sharp and shrill and mercifully short. Most would bob-tail off through the stubble, weaving and leaping as men whooped and yelled and dived upon them in their desperate flight, occasionally catching one to execute it with a swift, side-handed blow behind its ears, breaking its neck; for this was war-time and rabbits were standard fare.

The majority escaped the men but were not so lucky with the much swifter and deadlier dogs, Rex and Ruff; the latter the farm dog, a mongrel-mix of Old English sheepdog and less dominant genes. These two usually gentle canines reverted in an instant to their distant wolf ancestor, hurtling wildly, barking in high-pitched and murderous excitement after the rabbits which leaped and sprang and zig-zagged towards the hedgerow. Some would make it, spurting to sanctuary down a hole. Others, gained on by the dogs, were grabbed at the back of the neck by sharp, saliva-flecked fangs, and dog and prey, momentarily frozen in a daguerreotype, would tumble under an ancient and pitiless sun. Still others, panic-stricken, would be in survival distance of the hedgerow before abruptly and inexplicably about-turning, straight into the dogs' jaws.

The area of corn grew less, the earth began to spin away from the sun and the horses turned every few minutes until the last rabbit had bolted and the final sweep had been made. The binder was left in a corner of the field and Lion and Punch were released into the grass-meadow to graze peacefully, their body-steam dissipating in the cool of twilight. The sinking sun speared rays between the branches of hedgerow trees, and the midges began to bite. Birds sang their eventide song and a kestrel hovered above the field, eager for small rodents.

And tragedy unexpectedly struck.

"What's wrong wi' the dog?" someone said.

We all turned to look.

Rex had abruptly collapsed into the stubble, shaking violently.

"Ee's foamin' at the mouth, look!"

Mr Friend, looking anxious, moved to kneel beside him. "What is it, ol' bay?"

Others joined him.

"Ee's 'avin' a fit, be un?"

Rex's eyes had rolled back exposing just the whites. He emitted little yelps, his tongue lolled bright red. Suddenly his four limbs stiffened, trembling rapidly, he began to jerk, his chest jumped and heaved.

"Ee's 'avin' a fit for zure!"

But now he stilled, his chest stopped heaving and his legs lowered slowly to the ground. He ceased whimpering and his eyes clouded over, gradually, gently, closed to a slit. At first no one spoke. Mr Friend stroked his head. "Come on, ol' lad, buck up."

But Rex lay still.

Mr Friend remained silent, still stroking the old boy's head. Rex was motionless now. Life, when it deserts the body, takes its aura with it, leaving something less behind. You can always tell.

* * * * *

There was a sliver of moon, and stars like jewelled pendants on the soft satin of night, as I stood before my bedroom window. Below me, the aged plum tree beside our tottery garden gate coveted the honeyed bouquet of its own fruit within silent shadow, for the night was breezeless and fragrant. Starlight fell muted upon the dried-earthen path winding its way to the Friend's orchard.

A figure appeared, slightly bowed under the weight of a towel-wrapped burden, and a pang of melancholy struck me as, for a moment, a celestial light cosseted a canine head drooping lifelessly in its arms; for death then came still as a shock to me, a disturbing incomprehensibility.

I watched the forlorn figure of Mr Friend traverse the path and dissolve into shadow, before turning with heavy heart to my bed.

Rex was buried in a secluded corner beneath a craggy old tree which bore nectarous summer russets and would provide protection over his solitary resting place.

Ee wuz a guid ol' bay.

DENNIS

Dennis started school the same day as I did, left school the same day. We were contemporaries, but not friends; too different in personality and temperament. When, at the end of the war, Doris and Stacy were transferred to the newly-built secondary modern school in Torrington, Dennis and I walked home together, sometimes the shortest route for him, sometimes for me, both routes conjoining at Langham Cross. Often, we deviated from the road, exploring woods and tumble-down linhays in corners of fields, sagging and dangerous, long abandoned and left to rot. We would follow brooks into unknown terrain, hide in summer within stooks of drying corn.

The village dump, on our route, was bisected by a road, opposite which a mature beech wood climbed its steep slopes. This dump was a place of wonder, an Aladdin's cave of old bottles and cans and broken crockery; disposed-of furniture and other intriguing and unidentifiable items. The dump was vast, rising from the brook's bank to infringe the road. Acrid fumes hung permanently over the surface, vaporous spirals of smoke rose mysteriously here and there. Probe beneath this surface and it was a time capsule. Ancient artefacts lay long buried there, old medicine bottles from Victorian times, some still containing ancient potions. We would remove their rusted caps to release the dark and viscous contents, curdled and pultaceous, foul-smelling, from which we would reel back in delighted horror.

Deeper still, we would gaze into our excavated recesses as if into the entrance of Hades. Maleficent odours, wisps of ancient smoke like gaseous skeletal fingers, swirled and groped towards us. Occasionally a low rumble emerged, like the angry growl of a disturbed demon, and we would back sharply away. Sometimes we were still there when the school bus from Torrington rattled past, when we would hurriedly conceal ourselves lest Doris spot us and gleefully inform our parents that we'd been illicitly scavenging on the dump.

* * * * *

Being allowed to run free during the school dinner hour, one summer's day, Dennis and I crossed a stile and descended a field at the bottom of which Nippy

Bater, a grizzled and hirsute pensioner, had his allotment. Here were illicit riches which we often plundered; raspberry and blackcurrant canes heavy with plump and glistening fruit; sweet and tender carrots nestling in warm soil; sugary, succulent peas green as emeralds in their pods. I was first through the gate and had just plucked the first pea pod when there was a sudden roar and Nippy materialised from the hedgerow like the Wild Man of Borneo, waving a big stick.

He grasped me by the collar. "I'll teach ee, pinchin' me peas, you little 'eller!" His face was red, his drooping moustache bristling.

I cowered, terrified, turning to Dennis for support only to see the rear of him, legs pumping furiously back up the field.

Nippy was shaking me like a terrier with a rat. "You little divel, you, you'm lucky I don' clip ee round yer yur; box yer yurs, I should. You'm thiky Boxall bay, bain't ee? I know yer vather'n ee'll deal wi' ee, sure nuff ee will, I'll zee to that!" Another shake and my teeth rattled. "Now back to skewel wi' ee!" So saying, he pushed me out the gate.

I spent the rest of the afternoon frantic at what Dad would say, wishing Nippy had just boxed my ears and have done with it, not tell Dad. Dad was handy with a slipper on my backside when called for:

surely stealing peas must be worth a slippering? Even worse, being sent to bed with no tea.

Days passed. A low worm of dread haunted me, until one day Dad confronted me. "You'll come and apologise to Mr Bater," he said. "Stealing peas, indeed!" But I noticed just the hint of a grin: maybe fond memories of his own boyhood.

Oh, relief!

* * * * *

The legend of Dennis's boot: still talked of to this day.

By now six of us were attending primary school: myself; Valerie, my sister; Anne, our cousin; Christine, Archie Parkhouse's niece; and Trevor and Raymond from Westlake farm, all walking the same route home. Usually we walked the shortest route, West Lane, avoiding the dump on the Cleave Hill route.

West Lane was just that, a very narrow road sinking lower and lower between ever higher hedgerows with fields climbing on either side, streams sneaking from secretive places before swerving away into further inaccessible spots. In winter the hedgerows were skeletal, fields turned inside-out by the plough, brooks swollen and trees creating a drunken filigree against the sky. On these days we seldom lingered.

Come spring, life magically returned, snowdrops lined the brook like a carpet of green-tinted snow; later, primroses in clotted-cream clumps; tall daffodils, aloof and willowy in the breeze; finally bluebells, sapphire reflections of approaching summer.

Now we lingered, quibbling over wild strawberries, gurning grotesquely at the acrid, bitter tang of purple sloes we tortured ourselves by eating merely because they looked seductively luscious. We clambered to the top of a particularly steep field just to roll back down and stagger to our feet at the bottom, heads spinning, stomachs lurching, laughing queasily. We dammed streams, muddying ourselves in the process, just to see the dams breeched and tumbled, releasing a miniature tsunami. We cast sticks into an underwater conduit, rushing to see them appear on the other side like Pooh sticks.

During one exuberant tussling match, Anne's library book sailed high to entangle itself in overhead telephone wires, becoming droopier and sadder, until one windy night it became dislodged and Anne gingerly retrieved it from the gutter to shamefacedly return it.

* * * * *

Usually, Dennis took the Cleave Hill route home. On this particular day he accompanied us down West Lane and we lingered where a brook appeared briefly before veering off into thick scrubland. We decided to explore deeper, following the brook and thrashing our way along its nearside bank. Eventually, some now long-forgotten attraction on the far bank catching our eye, we decided to wade across. Dennis, who was wearing hob-nail boots, decided it would be easier to throw our footwear over first. But his own right-boot fell short, tumbling into the fast-flowing stream.

We watched in fascinated amusement, all except an appalled Dennis, as the boot rolled and tumbled rapidly downstream like some lumpen water creature until disappearing into the murky depths of a pool. We probed for it with long sticks, hoping to raise it, but all we raised was a swirl of mud, silt and blackened, decaying leaves. Eventually, with Dennis hopping woefully on one leg, we headed back to the lane.

"What be ee gwain'a do," we chortled.

By now, shuffling with one unshod foot, Dennis looked mortified.

"What will ee tell yer Mum?"

"I dunno … Er'll wallop me er weal, fer zure."

We all nodded sagely.

A look of hope suddenly appeared on Dennis's face. "Thure's one up een the cobblers," he exclaimed, "bein' repaired. Ee may be ready'n er'll vorget ee's there'n er'll never know what 'appened."

We all nodded; a little dubious but, not wanting to destroy his ray of hope, we agreed.

So off Dennis went, limping back up the lane wearing one boot. We watched silently until his dejected figure disappeared around a bend, when we all burst into uncontrollable laughter.

* * * * *

"Ow did ee get on?" we asked, the next day.

Dennis looked crestfallen.

"Did er notice?"

"Yeah, er did," Dennis said.

"Ow did er know?"

"Twas the zame boot," Dennis said, mournfully.

"What'd ee mean, the zame boot?"

"Zame boot; both boots was the zame right voot. Er noticed straight off."

"Oh." Trying to supress our glee.

"An' me bloomin' voot wus zore's 'ell time I got 'ome!"

"Really?"

"You bloomin' try wearin' yer right boot on yer left voot all the way 'ome!" exclaimed Dennis, indignantly.

We could contain ourselves no longer, all bursting into hysterical laughter.

* * * * *

"What wuz you little divels up to wi' Dennis's boot?" accused Dennis's mother, next Sunday: she was the week's Sunday school teacher. She was also loud, large, and overbearing.

We looked guileless, tried to keep straight faces.

"The bay's got a gurt blister on ee's voot, an' I've got'n odd boot now, an' I still owe the cobbler vive bob!"

We tried to avoid looking at each other, faces turning red, desperate to contain our laughter.

"What guid's one boot, I ask ee?"

A pause, then, "A spare…?" suggested Trevor.

That did it, and we all exploded into mad hilarity. Even Dennis joined in, then his mother.

* * * * *

On the day I betrayed Rachel I walked home with Dennis the West Lane route. As always, we lingered. We were building a dam across a roadside stream when Dennis looked up and said. "Thiky ol' maid's comin'."

I followed his gaze to see Rachel walking towards us; two or three years older now, her dark hair longer. She had a symmetrical face, pale and dark-eyed, was smartly dressed in Waddling's School uniform and carried a cluster of books under her arm.

"Thinks er's summin', look at er," sneered Dennis.

Waddling's private school inevitably evoked the class-war instinct in we Church School urchins, although Rachel's parents were a normal, small-farm family, who only wanted the best for their bright daughter.

But that carried no weight with Dennis.

I said nothing, but a shadow of concern loomed over me. I had not seen or spoken to Rachel since we vacated the village hall; I was no longer vulnerable and friendless, no longer an endearing infant. Memory of her friendship was growing hazy, but a sense of loyalty, of obligation, still remained within me.

Dennis stepped into the middle of the road, mud-smeared, dripping water and hair awry. Although not tall, he was stocky, solid; his somewhat moon-face, thin lips, and pale-grey eyes could look intimidating.

I saw Rachel falter slightly as she approached us.

"Where be you off to then, maid?" said Dennis, blocking her advance.

Rachel halted; taller than Dennis, elegant, slender. She didn't speak.

Dennis looked her up and down, scorn twisting his face. "I said, where be ee gwain?"

"Home," said Rachel, evenly. She looked at Dennis, did not glance at me standing uncomfortably to one side.

I hoped she didn't remember me. But I knew she did.

Dennis shuffled some more, puffed out his chest. "Home!" he scoffed, exaggerating the aitch with derision. "Home! Where's that, then?"

"Woolridge," replied Rachel, pausing before adding, "you know that."

We knew, of course we did; Woolridge Farm, above the valley on the Halsdon road.

Dennis shuffled some more. I could see his mind searching for something derogatory to say.

I glanced furtively at Rachel, but she was looking directly at Dennis, who was shuffling uncertainly now. "What've ee got there?" Nodding at Rachel's books.

"Homework."

"Omework!" scoffed Dennis. "Omework … Let's 'ave a look." He reached for them.

Now Rachel glanced directly at me, tightened her grip on the books, and I saw the fear in her eyes. I cringed, my stomach churning as guilt flooded over me. Still I said nothing: me, that sweet little boy she had taken so protectively under her wing. What must she think?

But she was gazing straight at Dennis again now. "I'd rather not," she said.

Was she waiting for me to come to her aid? Protect her as she had protected me? If so, she waited in vain.

I could see Dennis mustering the courage to snatch her books, cast them into the stream or some such.

Rachel could too, because she gripped them with both hands now, drew herself to her fullest height and darted quickly around Dennis who made to grab her, but backed away at the last minute, snatching a handful of sludge from the gutter and flinging it at her retreating back. I watched it splatter across her skirt, saw her flinch, but continue walking with quiet dignity. I felt a craven coward: I was a craven coward! A traitor.

"That'll teach er," said Dennis. "Posh blinker, thinks er's somethin' er does."

I said nothing.

"You reckon?" Dennis turned to me.

"I reckon," I said.

* * * * *

That was a long time ago. Rachel, if she is still alive, will be in her eighties now. I remember it still, and feel ashamed. After the betrayal I saw her occasionally, leaving Waddling's, around the village.

Ashamed, I avoided her. If she saw me, she never let on.

* * * * *

Occasionally I accompanied Dennis home to his family farm. There we explored the crepuscular barns and out-houses, where shafts of hazy sunlight penetrated fissures in the crumbling cob walls and vaulted thatched roofs supported by rough-hewn, centuries-old oak beams. Thick dust swirled and spun in a golden galaxy, falling upon farm implements and rusting machinery, now defunct, and bulging sacks of grain, some spilling their contents where rats and mice had filched their fill. These rodents we would glimpse momentarily before they scuttled, scally and hunched-backed, into darkened, straw-filled corners where we would hear them sniffling and skittering.

The farmhouse itself was old, centuries so. A cattle-shed was conjoined to it, separated only by an inner cob wall. A sour-sweet smell of cattle, suckling calves and corn-dust permeated the place. Overhead, the loft ran unobstructed the length of shed and house; barn owls nested there, leaving regurgitated pellets of compressed, de-sanguinated mice and voles; rats scuttled, and spiders lurked.

We decided one day to explore the loft to its full length. Brittle straw from long-past harvests crunched into dust under our feet, mantles of cobwebs brushed our faces as we ventured tentatively into murky, unexplored territory.

Then, without warning, a sharp crack, an explosion of pulverised plaster, and my left leg disappeared through a hole in the floor. I yelped in alarm and pulled back my leg, muted light accompanying it.

We peered wide-eyed down the hole.

"Cor, 'ell, tis the baidroom!" exclaimed Dennis in wonder.

I could see a large double bed with an eiderdown covered in powdered mortar and woodworm-riddled slats amidst a scattering of straw and rat droppings, a mummified rat, like a dead foetus. A cloud of rancid dust billowed upward, making us sneeze.

"Blinkin' 'ell!" I began to laugh.

Dennis's moon-face peered anxiously at me through the dust. "'Tis Mother's an' Vather's baidroom," he said.

I laughed louder. "What be ee gwain'a tell 'em?" I asked.

"Er'll drash me, fer zure," said Dennis, miserably.

"Tell 'em ..." I suddenly remembered that it was my foot which had done it. "No ... tell 'em ... I dunno."

"They'm bound to notice," mourned Dennis, peering woefully at dust now settling on the debris-strewn bed. "You reckon?" he asked, with fearful optimism.

"I reckon," I said. And giggled.

* * * * *

"You'm little divels, the pair'v ee!" ranted Mrs Harris. "What on earth do ee think you wuz playin' at?" She grabbed an anguished Dennis by his collar, shaking him violently. "Up to baid wi' ee an' stay thur an' don't think you'm comin' down to zupper, neither!"

She turned to me as I prepared to run. "And you, git on 'ome this instant an' I'll be tellin' yer vather, zure nuff I will, an' don't you thaink otherwise."

I scurried frantically away.

* * * * *

Dennis's lane was accessed by a single-track road winding its way down to Dolton Valley. It was also accessible by a short-cut, cutting at right-angles across a field from Dolton Cross.

Dennis and I stood gazing over the gate of this field at a flock of peacefully grazing sheep as a passing cloud rippled its shadow stealthily over them, creating a foam-flecked sea. "Thur's a ram een thur someplace," said Dennis, knowingly. "The beggar'll chase ee if'n ee zees ee, zure nuff ee wail."

We both scanned the grazing flock. "Can ee zee un?" I asked.

Dennis paused. "Beggar's thur someplace, fer zure," he said.

"P'raps us should go round the roadway," I suggested.

"Git out, you, us'll be over the field afore ee knows us is there."

"You reckon?" I said, warily.

But Dennis was already clambering over the gate, sheep bustling reluctantly away, fleece like snow-slush under the cloud-shadow.

"Ee'll butt ee, given 'alf a chance, mind," Dennis said, as we hurried furtively across the field. "Right divel, ee be."

I gazed uneasily around. "What's un look like?" I said.

"Big, wi' 'orns," said Dennis. "Ee've got 'orns." He grinned. "Bollocks, too," he said, "like turnips!"

We were more than halfway across the field, sheep demurring us passage, when, "Thur ee is!" shrilled Dennis.

I turned to see the ram standing rigid, several yards away, and staring straight at us. Even from this distance he resembled a horned devil, one foreleg stamping the earth. Then he charged like a woolly tank.

"Ooh, the 'eller's comin'!" wailed Dennis. And set off lickety-split for the far gate. It was Nippy Bater all over again; I was being abandoned!

I ran frantically, could hear the ground thudding behind me, and glanced back to see a massive beast bearing fast down upon us. Turf and sheep droppings flew from my heels as sheer terror caused me to gain upon Dennis. Another fleeting glance, and I saw the ram was gaining fast. He was close enough for me to hear his fiery devil's breathing. I threw myself at the gate, toppling Dennis who was already halfway over, sending us both tumbling in a heap on the far side.

There was a crunch of tortured wood as a fearsome horned head slammed into the gate. By the time we had disentangled ourselves, the beast was grazing a few feet back from the gate, its baleful eyes turned slyly upon us as if saying, "Nearly … Next time!"

We both rose to our feet and started to laugh, brushing ourselves down. "I told ee, ee wuz an 'eller, didn't I? I told ee zo!" exclaimed Dennis, triumphantly.

* * * * *

Dennis is dead now. He collapsed in a field with a heart attack aged sixty-five. Was lifted by Devon Air Ambulance to Barnstaple hospital; the first time he had flown. Seems poignant he wasn't in a fit state to enjoy it.

I went to his funeral in the little chapel cemetery. The chapel itself had been deconsecrated, was now a private residence. Times had changed. A lot. We mourners formed a circle at his graveside, the Methodist preacher read the liturgy. We sang hymns accompanied by a barrel organ and a banjo. Under a lowering sky a soft wind mourned with us. I glanced towards Mr Ford's grave. It was neglected, over-grown and lichen-covered.

The wake took place in Dolton village hall. After his mother's death, Dennis had neglected the already crumbling farmhouse to such an extent that he was living in a car. "Not a fit habitation any longer," his niece confided in me.

I met many people that day I had not seen for decades: pensioners now; evanescent shadows within which shimmered the essence of the children I had once known. Strangely comforting. A different world now. We were an intimate clique with shared and antiquated memories.

WE MOVE AGAIN

It was a wild day. Thunderclouds rolled over the horizon, seeming about to crash down upon us. Trees lashed and snapped in a sudden wind, their newly-sprung leaves trembling like emerald teardrops. Along the river bank daffodils intertwined like gold braid around a sea captain's cap. And today we were again moving house. Our new home was Rose Cottage: up the lane and over the brow of the hill from where Dartmoor could be seen brooding purple in the far distance, before swooping down again to Rose Cottage on the other side. Dad had already transferred the chickens and their coop, his tools and sundry equipment, and had now borrowed Tom and the cart to remove our furniture and belongings, necessitating several journeys.

Mr Friend helped him load up, with Tom hitched to a sturdy privet shrub beneath the old plum tree. Squalls of icy rain like biting nails were interspersed by short sunny spells when the countryside hesitantly smiled.

"Careful with that, Bill," said Mum, anxiously, gazing at the tilting china cupboard.

"I know what I'm doing, Eed," said Dad, his tone brittle.

"'Tis okay, don't ee worry, missus," said Mr Friend, cheerily.

"It's delicate," said Mum, unconvinced. A gust of wind chittered the leaves, plump raindrops splattered spitefully on Tom's rump, and with the wind came a ghostly howling; distant, rising, falling.

Tom's ears pricked up, he shook his head and whinnied, his large hooves vibrated the ground and his rump swayed.

The rain passed; a break in the wind. The howling was nearer now, sharper and tinged with menace.

Tom shuffled harder. He began to toss his head, jerking the tether. His eyes rolled back, exposing the whites. The cart creaked, jolted, the steel-rimmed wooden wheels groaned.

"Bugger me if tidn' the 'ounds!" exclaimed Mr Friend. "You'll 'ave to watch the beggar now, sure nuff." He clutched Tom's reins at the head. "Steady now, steady!" he barked.

Tom whinnied again; the baying of fox-hounds rose and fell like ocean rollers as Mr Friend and Dad manoeuvred our Calor gas stove onto the cart and lashed it down firm.

"That'll do for this load, I reckon," said Mr Friend. "Better get off afore the 'ounds get any closer."

The baying abruptly exploded in intensity; the shrill blast of a hunting horn cut through the air like a scimitar.

Tom lunged backwards, whinnying louder. The privet shrub was wrenched like a groaning tooth from the hedge, its serpentine roots cracked and split, spraying stones and clods of earth. On the cart, Dad swayed and staggered as the multifarious cargo tinkled, jiggled and clattered alarmingly. Mr Friend disentangled the shattered privet shrub from the tether and backed Tom around towards the lane, the cart creaking in tortured protest.

"'Old they reins firm now, Beal," he said, and off we went, myself having scrambled onto the cart – being required to help Dad unload – Dad, standing wedged against the kitchen table, leaning back on the reins holding Tom in check and shouting harshly at him. The old horse seemed transformed, neck arched, mane flying, hooves zipping aside stones as if from a slingshot. I held grimly on to the juddering, bouncing gas stove, every jolt of the tyreless wheels on the stony lane scrambling my insides as we descended the other side far too fast. Tom's hooves slithered and skidded, his flanks sank low as the cart's shaft and Tom's forequarters rose, and Dad paled alarmingly, heaving back on the reins. "Whoa now, whoa! Calm down, damn you!"

Somehow Tom righted himself, the cart bucking perilously, the cacophony of its contents a discordant jazz arrangement, before it gained an even keel.

We crossed the tarmacked road at the end of the lane and Dad jumped from the cart to grab Tom's bit for the descent to Rose Cottage, the lane being hazardously steep and pitted. (Occasionally, delivery vans were driven down it against all advice to the contrary, only to have to await a tractor, driven by a grinning farmer, to haul them back up).

The sounds of the hunt were now deadened by the hill behind us, and Tom calmed as Dad cautiously piloted him down the lane, hooves skidding and gouging into the stony earth, holding back. By the time we reached the bottom he had reverted to his normal placid self and stood sweating and snorting, nibbling the lane-side grass as we unloaded with the thunderclouds hovering over us like Hades' angels. By the time we returned with the last load, they had burst their skins to drench us in their lifeblood, and we spent the first hours in our new home miserably chilled to the bone until Mum got a fire going to heat some bath water.

Miraculously the china cupboard had remained intact.

* * * * *

Rose Cottage lay across the ridge and deeper in the valley than Brightly. On clear days and up the valley, Dartmoor could be seen rising mauve against a clear washed-blue sky and from which sometimes, on winter days, a wind the colour of mercury and with sharp teeth swept down upon us.

It was a thatched cottage with walls of thick cob. Under its eaves sparrows nested, house martins returned each spring to nest directly above its front door; a door around which presumably roses had once grown; a sizable garden with fruit trees and a tall conifer which doubled as an aerial pole for our battery-powered wireless. Water was gravity-fed from a small reservoir in the field above, so at least Mum now had water on tap. Mr Dutton however, had had an extension added with another bedroom, toilet, and bathroom. The original fireplace had been bricked up and a small grate installed with a back boiler for hot water, so luxury indeed: a flush toilet and a real hot-water bath! Even in Surrey we had only had a tin bath.

The previous owner, Miss Bingham, a solitary spinster, a long-ago debutante who had presumably fallen upon hard times (this was long before the time of holiday cottages or second homes), had died in the main bedroom. Valerie and I had run the odd errand for her, collected firewood. She had been kind to us, given us a half-crown for our help, gave us Christmas presents. She had once shown us a photo of herself, a sepia print of a young and pretty girl in a grand garden and flanked on either side by a regal-looking wolfhound. She must have given us some potted history of herself, but no memory of it remains with me if she did. Cruelly, we used to laugh at her behind her back, at her refined accent, her rather gushing personality. On our last visit she did not answer the door; we could hear her moaning in pain in the bedroom above and we never saw her again.

On our first day in the cottage we chased around the bedroom moaning exaggeratedly, "Ohoooa! We're Miss Bingham's ghost ... ohoooa," before it suddenly dawned upon me that maybe her ghost really was there! Other ghosts, too, saturated with them in this ancient room with its sagging low ceiling, creaking floorboards and uneven cob walls, its small latticed window set deep in a shadowy aperture. How many other people had died here over the centuries? "I bags the new bedroom," I said quickly. And because it was smaller, was allowed it. Valerie had the tiny box room.

Above the landing outside my bedroom was a trapdoor entrance to the loft which extended over both new and old sections. None of us had ever ventured up there. Occasionally at night I heard scuffling noises, patterings, a shuffling in the eaves, and tried not to think of ghosts; just the nesting sparrows.

One summer's evening I pulled back my sheets and leapt back in horror. An insect, striped black and yellow, as thick as my thumb and pulsing rhythmically, rested upon my pillow. It hummed softly.

"Mu-um!"

But Dad appeared. "A hornet," he said, "nasty sting. Lucky you saw it," and he threw a towel over it to remove it.

There were more after that; we saw them droning peacefully around the fruit trees, in the kitchen. "Shoo, shoo!" Mum would exclaim, waving a tea towel and preparing to run. "Don't go near it, duck, it stings."

Shinnie Mead, the village builder, was on the roof one day repairing a crack in the chimney stack when one became trapped up his trouser leg and stung him. Twice. Shinnie was a big man, but he still ended up for a day in Torrington Cottage Hospital.

"I've seen them going up under the thatch," said Dad. "They must be in the attic." Using a stepladder he warily lifted the trapdoor and peered in. There, in the gloomy recess above my bedroom was a symmetrical wonder, a huge and delicate, beautiful wedding cake, throbbing mellifluously: the hornet castle.

Dad called a pest controller in to remove it. A shame, I thought; it was their home and generally they cohabited peacefully with us. But they did have a nasty sting.

Our days in Rose Cottage were generally happy. Mum and Dad were still young, Valerie and I were still children, the war was over and material conditions were gradually improving; sweets were off ration and comics were in colour.

MICKY

Micky came to us one summer holiday. Valerie and I with our cousin Anne went to collect him from the Old Rectory at Huish where he had been delivered, just weaned, from Torrington, the tiny product of a spaniel and a Labrador belonging to the town's ironmonger.

We went by the old road, long abandoned since the laying of the tarmacked road on the advent of the motor car, and now a stony lane winding tranquilly between woodlands of stately oak and beech. The hawthorn, blackthorn, ash, hazel, and elder hedgerows were awash with summer seas of umbellifers and red campion, the colourful pink and purple of the labiate family, and wild, fragrant orchids; honey bees and bumble bees, wood-wasps, and butterflies; a kaleidoscope of pastel colours shimmering and swaying in tree-filtered sunlight. Scents drifted down the lane in an olfactory river.

Reaching the lane's apex we emerged into full sunlight. The estate's lordly mansion could be glimpsed in the distance between tall grasses, thickets, and groves, beyond which an amethyst sky met the earth.

We entered the Old Rectory courtyard to see a tiny black bundle, all feet and ears and curious eyes, still nervous without his mother, outside the kitchen door. Spotting us oohing and aahing and rushing towards him, he turned tail and bolted on unsteady feet back indoors. Once introduced to us however, recognising us as friends, he jumped up and licked us ingratiatingly, rolled onto his back exposing a pink and soft warm tummy for us to tickle, before struggling to his feet again.

On the way home we took it in turns to carry him, let him walk a little way, sniffing uncertainly at this strange and vast new world he had entered. The sun beamed down, and the birds sang, the perfumed breeze was soft and warm on our faces and the day sparkled as we again reached the high place of tall grass and dominant sky. The world at that moment was an enchanted place indeed.

* * * * *

That same year Puss died. She was only six and had led a varied and not pain-free life: while still at

Brightley had vanished for six weeks and we had thought never to see her again, but one day she returned, dragging a near-severed back leg behind her.

"Must've been a gin trap, looks like," Dad said, the leg connected by only a thin strip of skin. But it was not generally the practice to call in a vet back then, only for livestock; pets had to take their chances. At least, they did where we lived. Presumably some of the more sensitive village folk did, of course, and now years later I feel guilty. But I was only eight and I guessed Dad couldn't afford it, because he was not an uncompassionate man. Either way, the leg soon dropped off of its own accord, the stump healed over, and Puss continued the same loving and friendly cat as ever. Occasionally she would accidentally knock the stump, when she would hiss and circle until the pain subsided. But she still trusted me to pick her up, fuss over her and put her on my lap, always careful not to nudge the stump.

A couple of times a year she would give birth to a litter of kittens; once, in the farm cart shed, from whence she gently transported them home one by one in her mouth, only for Dad to take and kill them by a sharp crack on their tiny heads. Unwanted farm cat litters were routinely drowned in the nearest water butt, but Dad considered this cruel. Callous it may now seem, but times were different then, harder, post-war austerity was rampant, money and materials were in short supply.

For a few days, Puss would meow and anxiously search for her lost litter, before settling down with the one survivor Dad always allowed her. When weaned, the survivor would be given to anyone who wanted a cat, but most would end up being transported in Dad's haversack to Huish and released at Home Farm, where they would take their chances amongst the other rodent-controlling farm felines.

Puss moved with us to Rose Cottage where she gave birth to one last litter and was again allowed one last survivor, which Valerie and I named Nickolas-Thomas after a story-book kitten on *Children's Hour*.

Up to this point Puss and Nickolas-Thomas had slept indoors. But then had come Micky, a brazen and friendly puppy, and Puss had taken umbrage to this upstart intruder who, being a puppy, just wanted to play with her. She would hiss and snarl and lash out at him, so Dad arbitrarily banned her and her kitten from the house. Mum supplied them with a cardboard box for a bed, which she placed under an old outdoors table. But soon came autumn and with it came cold winds and questing rain and an epidemic of cat flu. Nickolas-Thomas died first, a half-grown bundle of fur curled into himself. A few days later I came home from school to be informed by Mum that Puss had died. I went to see her, curled up calm and peaceful as if asleep. But when I gently stroked her, she felt cold and somehow not there anymore; not our warm and loving Puss. I shed a few tears before going indoors to play with our new puppy.

We buried Puss under an apple tree in the chicken run at the bottom of our garden. I never thought to give her a marker, and her grave soon became nothing more than a muddied hollow in the ground where she joined Mr Ford as a fading memory.

Only many years later, after Dad's death, did Mum remark that it had been wrong, Dad shouldn't have exiled Puss like that; she was only behaving as cats do and it *was* her home after all, and he shouldn't have done it. By then I was in my forties and it hit me suddenly, shocking me that I didn't at least try to dissuade Dad; maybe let her sleep in my bedroom away from Micky or something. She was my cat and I betrayed her just as I had betrayed Rachel years before, and I belatedly said a silent prayer for Puss's long departed soul.

* * * * *

From his progenitors Micky had inherited a consummate sense of smell. Often on walks we would wait until he was distracted by something, a rabbit maybe, when we would quickly dash away and hide behind a tree or bush. Realizing we had vanished, Micky would return to the spot he had last seen us, instantly pick up our scent and unhesitatingly nose to the ground, track us unerringly to our hiding place.

When he outgrew puppyhood, he was installed in a kennel Dad had had made for him and tethered to a long chain a few feet from our front door. This didn't however preclude him from spending a substantial time indoors with us.

He hated to be left alone and we went to great, almost comical, extremes to avoid him knowing we had all gone out: we would pretend to be particularly active and noisy, never let him see us in going-out clothes before sneaking out the back door and up the lane. He wasn't fooled though, always knew, saw through the charade, and before we even reached the top of the lane he would begin to whine anxiously.

Not that we went out together often, maybe to Dolton 'pictures' in the village hall on Saturday nights, or a social evening, never for more than four or five hours. Other than that, one or other of us was always at home with him. But he did come to church with us, not that we went every Sunday, but on fine summer's evenings when mist gathered over the river and hedgerow scents lay heavy in the air, stooked corn spread a golden haze over the fields and heat shimmered above the country roads.

"Love me, love my dog," Dad was fond of saying. Or, in this case, "We come to church? The dog comes too."

Our nearest church was four miles or so distant and it did not seem right Micky not walking with us on tranquil summer evenings.

"He's one of God's creatures and he's welcome," said the vicar, seeming a little dubious, but intimidated by Dad's forthright manner and, as the church was situated in a tiny hamlet as deep in the countryside as it was possible to get, four extra in the congregation was no mean gain.

And so Micky settled quietly at the end of a pew and dozed with the rest of us through the sermon. The vicar was gentle and grey, growing weary and one of the old-school. The church too; its centuries-old pews worn and riddled by departing woodworm (God's creatures?). Built of granite, it seeming to be slowly and gratefully settling into the soft grass along with its surrounding graves of country ancients, long departed. House martins crossed thousands of miles from the dark continent, unerringly returning to nest in its porch, honey bees nested in its weathered walls, and its tower housed bats and jackdaws, all God's creatures, welcome or not. In its windbreak trees was a rookery, the denizens of which quarked and grated querulously, dark angels circling and swooping over the church. It is still there, still hidden and remote.

* * * * *

If a bitch was on heat at some distant farm or cottage Micky always knew; an absolute mystery to us. Dad, having been reared under strict Victorian morals, and having a thing about sex, which inexplicably extended to dogs and animals in general, was angrily aroused at any sign of sexual agitation in Micky. He would berate him sternly, ensure he was always securely chained up. But sometimes, through sheer sexual frustration and delirium, Micky would flagrantly disobey him, somehow slipping his lead and slithering fox-like over the hedge and up the lane, for all the world like an escapee from the dog pound, ignoring Dad's infuriated, roared demands that he return immediately.

Dad, who hated disobedience from any of us ("You dare disobey me!") would utter dire threats and mutter his disgust at this sordid and blatant display of sexual degeneracy. "Don't let me catch you with girls before you're seventeen," he would exclaim to me on some whim and for no apparent reason, therefore arousing my nascent sexual instincts.

Micky would eventually return, muddy and dishevelled, tail between his legs, eyes full of guilt, and crouch low in front of Dad in full subjugation. "Into your kennel!" Dad would roar. "And stay there." And so he did, subdued and looking pathetically sorry for himself.

How successful his philanderings were we never knew or discussed: were there any Mickylets around in some far-flung farmyard?

Nevertheless, he was a much-loved dog by all of us, and a faithful companion. In his early years he would accompany me and my friend Trevor on our explorations and adventures. In his middle years, after I had left home, he faithfully accompanied Valerie on her long, solitary walks. In his autumn years, Valerie having married and left home, and Mum and Dad now settled in a bungalow (with electricity!) in a neighbouring village, he became obsessively attached to them, and terribly upset should one or the other of them not be with him at all times.

By now, of course, his kennel was long abandoned, and he was living indoors. Dad had an old butcher's-boy bicycle with a large iron-framed basket attached to its handlebars into which Micky would clamber and ride off to Huish, a good three miles away, to work and back with Dad every day.

On my naval leaves I would take him for walks, but the old exuberance had by now gone and the walks grew shorter each leave, dwindling eventually to just a short walk around the churchyard.

Looking back, I feel it strange that, even though the old dog was obviously ill in his final months and by then they could have afforded it, they never took him to a vet.

They got up one morning to find him dead under the kitchen table. Dad buried him in a corner of the garden beneath a camellia shrub.

Author and Valerie outside Brightley Lodge circa 1943

Mum and Author pushing Valerie in pushchair accompanied by a young Puss circa 1943

Brightley House circa 1944

Mum and Auntie Ena at door of Brightley Cottage circa 1946

From left to right: Mum, cousin Brian, Author, Auntie Ena, and Valerie, circa 1946

Rose Cottage

Author, Valerie and cousin Brian circa 1946

Trevor and twin lambs

South approach to Sheepwash

The Boxall family at Anstey's Cove, Torquay circa 1952

CHARLIE

Something black in the field, down by the riverbank, something alive, stumbling and fluttering ragged against the green grass, and vaguely sinister. Micky, snuffling merrily, tail looping, spotted it and veered towards it, circling it warily as it shuffled jerkily away from him. It stopped suddenly, aware escape was impossible, reared clumsily up, a large, grey-pouched beak opening defiantly towards its tormentor. It was a rook, I could see now, obviously injured in some way.

As I approached it, it turned its head to face this new threat, ebony eyes glinting fiercely, coal-black wings splayed either side of it across the grass, like a vampire's cloak. It looked disturbingly big. A blue-black tongue slithered slug-like from the open beak and I backed off a way. Sensing nemesis delayed, it flapped away again, its wings like feathered oars rowing against the grass. Micky leaped at it playfully, then bounced back again, barking shrilly.

"Mick, leave!" I shouted. The rook was scurrying up the sloping meadow now, seeking some kind of sanctuary. Unable to fly, it wouldn't last long, would die slowly of hunger or thirst: that's if it wasn't first discovered by a fox or some other predator. Either way, an inevitable and miserable death awaited it. Should I somehow put it out of its misery? But how? It had reached the top of the meadow now, Micky and I right on its heels. Spotting a hedgerow rabbit's burrow as an escape route, it tried in desperation to enter it, and I saw my chance. With that large and menacing beak vanished down the hole, talons scrabbling for traction, it was temporarily defenceless.

Swiftly, I bent and clasped its wings gently but firmly against its body and withdrew it from the burrow. It tucked its neck between head and body, turned black inscrutable eyes upon me, opened its beak and hissed. But I could see it was resigning itself to whatever fate awaited it. Talons curled tightly around my fingers, I could feel rough scales rubbing against them and felt a brief moment of revulsion, a desire to drop it. The moment passed, and I turned it at an angle to see one talon had what appeared to be a bulbous growth upon it.

The bird struggled lamely, counteracted the turn to straighten its head. It was breathing heavily, and I could feel its heart beating like a tiny pulse against my palm, the down of its under-feathers warm and soft.

"What's wrong with you?" I asked. "You hurt your wing?" It was no longer using its beak as a threat, but half-closed, tongue moving with its heartbeat as it gazed steadily up at me. "What am I going to do with you?" I asked, gazing back at it. "Can't just leave you here, can I, seeing as you can't fly?"

Micky, who had been regarding my captive quizzically, finally lost interest and went off to snuffle for rabbits.

"I'll have to take you home, I reckon. Put ee in a box or something, 'til you'm better – or die." Which I knew from experience was what wild things usually did when captive; seemed to lose hope and will themselves to die. So off we went, back along the riverbank under whispering hazel and elder, across marsh-bordered meadowland where numerous wolf spiders bred profusely and contentedly amidst hummocks of coarse and tangled grass, undisturbed by plough or cattle; then across a skittish stream, up a steep meadow where rabbit droppings lay lavish, over a tumbled stone wall by which a proud young oak grew, and through our garden gate.

By now the rook had settled in my grasp, head cocking occasionally, gazing longingly, I imagined, at the overhead trees where shards of sunlight dazzled and danced. The family were seated at dinner. They looked up curiously at me standing in the doorway.

"I found un," I said, before they had chance to ask. "Ee can't fly."

"Well, what do you expect to do with it?" asked Dad.

"I dunno …" I gazed down at the rook, stilled in my grasp, eyeing the proceedings. "Found un down een Baily's marsh." And I went on to explain what had happened. "Couldn't just leave un there to starve, or for foxes to get, could I?" Valerie was on her feet now.

"P'raps ee's hungry," she said, and advanced towards me with some mashed potato from her plate in her open palm, extending it to the bird. To the surprise of all of us it didn't hesitate, but plucked eagerly at the offering, gulping it down.

"Must be really hungry," said Dad. "Better take it outside, it can't stay in here. Outside, I gingerly placed it on the lawn as Valerie put the remainder of the mash in front of it. It fluttered sideways, wings spread across the grass. One wing dragged uselessly. Then turned to the food and gobbled it up, glancing briefly up at us before flapping crab-like away across the garden. I strode to pick it up, emboldened now.

It turned its head to me, beak open in now only half-hearted threat. We fed it some more, then at Dad's suggestion, put it into a spare raised hutch in the chicken run.

"It's been shot," he said. "Got some pellets embedded in it, I reckon. It might survive. It's up to you, if you want to look after it." I did.

"Charlie," I grinned, as Valerie placed some more food into its hutch. "That's what us'll call un, Charlie." So Charlie it was. We passed more scraps of leftover dinner to it but, sated now, it had flapped into a corner and squatted watching us.

Next morning, before the school bus, I approached it apprehensively, half expecting to find it crumpled dead in the corner. But no, it had changed position and gazed beadily at me, then hopped, one wing dragging, to devour some stale soaked bread I placed in the hutch. So Charlie remained. We fed him every day before we went to school and again when we came home; left-over food scrounged from the table; chicken food. Any mice caught in traps I fed him too, and he devoured them solicitously whilst always remaining aloof and threatening me with his beak if I attempted to pick him up. Occasionally he would attempt to fly, but quickly flopped down again to the floor of his hutch.

I had an idea. I cut some long hazel and ash wands from the hedge and fabricated an elongated, ladder-like structure in the chicken run which would allow him to hop higher, to about five feet above the ground, rung by rung, which he did happily, perching jauntily upon the top rung.

He was with us for about five months, until one frosty winter's morning, before school, I went in semi-darkness to feed him as usual, only to find him dead in the corner of his hutch. It was sad, but I did not cry; well, maybe a sneaky tear. He was only a rook after all, and I'd done all I could for him. But I still carried a weight in my chest at school all that day. Well, he *had* been *my* rook. Me and Valerie buried him beside the chicken shed, and sometimes over the years we would look at the muddied spot and remember ol' Charlie.

SALLY

Sally came to us by rail. Early one autumn's day, with the beech leaves golden, the oak secreting fawn-brown acorns neat in their pitted cups, ash and sycamore keys spinning earthward in a balmy light breeze, and grasses in the wayside hedgerows long and fecund and rustling quietly, Dad and I cycled four or so miles along deserted country roads under a washed-blue sky to collect her from our nearest railway station outside a neighbouring village; single-track, field-and-woodland enshrouded and snaking ever deeper into the countryside.

We planted our bicycles against the station fence and walked into the tiny compact office and waiting room. Excitement, which had been welling within me on the ride, threatened to bubble over as Dad announced our mission.

"Oh, aye, tis yur sure nuff." The stationmaster, proudly clad in his dark-blue serge uniform, winked at me as he addressed Dad. "Would ee believe I've never seen one o' they afore?" he said, gazing at the small cage amongst the collection of railway cargo behind him. "Cute little devil, bain't un?" He turned to me. "Yours, I reckon?"

I nodded, staring happily at the plump, sandy-red-coloured creature crouched inside the cage. Its belly pulsed rapidly and its whiskers, on a long, largish face, twitched anxiously as it gazed warily at me through dark, beady eyes.

"Sally," I said proudly.

"Come a long way, 'ave un?" asked the stationmaster, eyeing the chewed-down carrot and shredded cabbage leaf inside the cage.

"Three hundred miles, give or take," said Dad.

All the way from Surrey, I knew, where we had been on holiday visiting Mum's and Dad's relatives with excursions to Hampton Court, Kingston-upon-Thames, and a battered post-war London – and most thrilling of all for me, the wondrous cinemas. They showed films of cowboys and Indians; of a wildman named Tarzan who swung on trailing vines through the jungle, and who lived in a tree house with a shapely, smooth-skinned mate called Jane. I had fallen in love with Jane.

"An old school-mate of mine," expanded Dad, "keeps racing pigeons and several guinea pigs." He nodded at Sally, then at me. "He adored them," he explained, "so Arthur promised to send him one."

And here she was. Sally.

✵ ✵ ✵ ✵ ✵

We cycled home along sun-baked roads with Sally in her cage fastened onto the carrier of Dad's bike with me just behind to make sure it stayed secure.

Dad had made a hutch ready for her, raised on stilts and just outside the chicken run, hay-lined and fronted with chicken-wire and a wooden door.

She bustled to the rear of the cage as I reached for her, little feet scrabbling futilely on the wooden base as I gently lifted her out. Her belly was soft and warm as a cushion against my palms as I clasped her to my chest before placing her into her new home, where she scrambled for safety into the hay, bunched roof-high at the back.

The weeks, the years, passed, and Sally remained as shy as ever. I fed her before I left for school and again when I returned home; carrots, cabbage leaves, dandelions, and groundsel which she seemed to love. She would emerge timidly from her nest of hay, nose twitching as I opened her hutch door, grab whatever delicacy I placed just inside, and scurry with it back to her nest. Twice a week or more,

I would replace her hay with fresh which I had snitched from a hayrick in a corner of a nearby field. Never seeming to wholly trust me, she always retreated timidly to the rear of her hutch, and I had to reach in and gently drag her out. I left her in the care of Valerie, who cooed and fussed over her, allowing her to scramble around under her jumper while I cleaned out her accommodation. Retrieving her from my reluctant sister, I returned her to the hutch, where she would burst from my grasp to vanish into the fresh hay.

A couple of years later, having left school and obtained a job on a local farm, I would pause on my cycle ride home to extract the largest and juiciest-looking dandelion I could see in the hedgerow.

"Here, Sal," I would say to the pair of gleaming eyes I could see peering at me through the hay. "Yur's a lovely milkydashal for ee."

And she would shoot out to drag it back into her nest.

Winter came and went, Charlie died, and I would worry about Sally. On frosty nights of silvery moonlight with stars like gems of ice, I would approach her hutch, always having made sure she had extra hay and ample food. "You alright, Sal?" There would be a brief rustle deep in the hay. "Good. Okay, then."

Sometimes a fox would screech, banshee-like in the nearby woods, a tawny owl would hoot mournfully. Once, a barn owl soared low over the garden like a snow-blown ghost, while the firs beyond the river rose Stygian-dark against a velvet sky. And knowing Sally was okay, I would return to the cosy, lamp-lit warmth of Rose Cottage with its glittering, rime-frosted thatch, and thick cob walls, where I would shiver in the glacial air before closing the door on the hostile night.

Timid, plump, and warm, she was still with us when some time later I left to join the Royal Navy.

"Don't forget to feed Sal," I reminded Valerie, "and to clean out her hutch a couple of times a week."

Some months later, while I was in the boys' huts of Devonport Naval Barracks, I received a letter from Dad. Sally had died. He had buried her at the base of the hedge beside her hutch. Mind, she had lived a long life for a guinea pig, he said, as if to comfort me. And I experienced a pang of sorrow deep in my chest, a wave of nostalgia for my home, a surge of love for the plump little guinea pig I had known.

Only later, on home leave, did Dad tell me that a rat had climbed a leg of her hutch and forced its way in, killing her by biting her throat. Why? I've no idea. Why anything? When it boils down to it there are no happy endings. There were none for the rat, either. Dad had laid a rat trap below the hutch the day after Sally's death, and had caught it, smashing it over the head with a stick.

"I made sure it saw it coming," he said. "For Sally."

PIGEONS

The pigeons came a year after Sally. In the centre of the station waiting room, the pot-bellied iron stove quivered within an aura of its own heat, radiating warmth. Outside, across the single-track line, a giant tangle of rhododendron shrubs seemed a viridescent, ruby-dotted wave about to break over the far platform.

"You'm startin' a menagerie, I reckon, looks like," grinned the stationmaster. He seemed to have gotten plumper since last time we'd seen him, his uniform tighter; a little dustier, too. "What's it gwain'a be next yur, I wonder, ferrets?"

Dad laughed. "Ferrets? No, pigeons and guinea pigs is enough," he said.

So we took the wicker basket containing six pigeons and strapped it to Dad's carrier. I could glimpse them shuffling around inside, like a surreal pastel painting in vivid motion, hear them cooing, smell them. Dad wobbled a bit as we moved off, the wicker basket, larger than Sally's had been, seemed to temporarily put him off balance. I hoped he wouldn't fall. Worried about harming the pigeons.

An October sun was lowering in the sky, playing peek-a-boo behind cumulus clouds like regal galleons and, in that unique October light, green fields and ruby-red cattle, milk-white sheep, were all somehow more intense, visually enhanced. The air held the approaching spirit of winter, a quicksilver effervescence. Everything appeared suddenly, vitally alive.

In our valley the sun had already reclined into a pink lake behind the fir forest and a sliver of mist coiled over the river, an ethereal pennant transiting the hollow. We traipsed down the steep lane, too stonily precipitous to ride a bike, and carried the restless, disoriented pigeons up to the chicken run where a galvanized, makeshift shed was to be their new home. Once inside, careful to close the wire-mesh door behind us, we released them. A scrabble of wings fluted the dusty air around us, and we flinched and blinked against it as the birds, cooing angrily amidst a farrago of downy feathers, sought a perch. Finding old chicken ones, a couple of rickety shelves, they eventually settled irritably down, eyeing us suspiciously.

"We'll leave 'em be, sort themselves out," said Dad. "They'll soon go to roost now, anyway. Have to keep 'em in for a while, till they accept this as their new home." And so we went, sliding quickly through the door before fastening it securely.

Next morning, laden with a bowl of grain, I peered eagerly into their shed. They were perched calmly; some on perches, a couple on the shelves. I saw now, in the clear light, that some were dusty-blue, others fawny-brown. Opening a small trapdoor in the wire mesh, I thrust through an arm holding the bowl and scattered the contents onto the floor. The pigeons quickly descended upon it, eating eagerly. I watched a while as they ate, feeling exquisitely proud as their owner and guardian.

Days grew shorter, nights longer. Winter's rimed fingers skittered up the valley, scritched flowery frost patterns on my bedroom window, and it became torment to arise from my womb-warm bed for school in the mornings. I worried now about the pigeons.

"They'll be alright," Dad assured me. "Same as the chickens, the wild pigeons, they're different from us."

Over the following weeks I came to know them as individuals but did not name them, only referring to them as 'the pigeons'. The cock strutted his masculinity, the hens studiously ignoring him, fluttering irritably out of his way. Every Saturday morning I would brave the cold to clean out their shed as they fluttered noisily around me. The cock flapped to settle on my back as I bent shovelling up the damp sludge of droppings and discarded grain husks. There, he haughtily swaggered, King of the Castle, dipping and cooing, proclaiming his bravura to the hens. Amused, I accommodated him submissively until he decided to jump off. It was then I thought to call him 'Father'.

* * * * *

In early January, "Seems like snow," observed the local farm workers, sagely, sniffing the air.

"Aye, tis comin'," it was agreed, "sure nuff."

And a tingle of excitement threaded down the spines of we children. Snow; frozen blocked roads; school bus couldn't get through; illicit, school-free days. Heaven!

Then one magical morning, there it was! Blanketing the garden, a glistening fairyland where yesterday were fields; trees like Arctic aliens, thick snow vaulting their boughs. Snow had built up a little at the base of the pigeon shed, softened the wire mesh to chequered squares. I peered through. They were perched fluff-feathered, looking fat.

"Bus didn't come," I told them, gleefully. As I opened the door to pass them extra grain, tiny landslides of snow fell silently from the wire. "Gonna go sledging, me'n Trevor be," I informed them, as they fell upon the grain.

* * * * *

By mid-January it had thawed. The countryside now looked sadly prosaic, soggy grey-green under a drab sky, and school seemed almost inviting; warm classrooms and cosily animated children.

One bright Sunday in February, brittle sunlight tinselling hedgerow and grass, charming the trees and greeting the first primroses to raise their clotted-cream heads in joyous salutation, Dad said, "It's time, I reckon, to free the pigeons." So, excited but with a sprinkling of fear, I watched as he opened wide their shed door before we both retreated a pace. Would they fly off over the fir forest never to return? Vanish for ever into the great blue yonder?

There was a hiatus, a frozen moment, as we stared at each other. Then, as if by telepathic consent and in a precipitation of sound and feathers, they flew from several weeks of confinement into freedom. Head back, eyes wide, I gazed in awe as they cannoned into the sky, tacking smoothly, elegantly to the left, soared high into the ice-blue yonder in perfect symmetry with each other before dipping sharply over the river. Dad and I, swinging to follow their circuit, saw them like mercurial rockets outlined against the dark forest before they planed high, soared until they were dark blots against the sky, then lost them in the sun. Squinting, we turned away, gazing from the corners of our eyes to see them emerge from the dazzle, angle low above their shed in their now one-hundred-and-eighty-degree orbit, where they lifted and hovered momentarily before repeating their cycle. Again we followed their curve, a manoeuvre which they repeated several times, then descending to hover briefly before landing in a rather confusing efflorescence of dust and feathers on the shed roof. They had come home, and my heart had soared with them.

From then on they were free to come and go at will, only shut in at nights because of foxes and rats. I never tired of watching their soaring, swooping circuits. Sometimes they dipped below the trees or below the rim of the valley, only seconds later to bloom again like clay pigeons from a catapult. They would land on the roof where, feathers ruffled, Father would stoop and bob and berate his harem, cooing authoritatively as the hens dodged disdainfully away. I always felt a warm glow at their accepting trust in me. This was their home now.

* * * * *

One Sunday a few weeks later, Dad said, "We'll toss the pigeons – not too far, but a few miles away."

"You think they'll find their way back?" I asked, unsure.

"They will. Pigeons do," said Dad.

I wasn't convinced. I didn't want to lose them.

"Trust me," said Dad.

The sun was in ascendency now, primroses dotting the hedgerows in splashes of buttercream, daffodils lining the riverbanks with golden battalions, and leaves bursting from bud like emerald damselflies. In those days there was little traffic on Devon's byroads, and Dad and I, the pigeons in their basket, cycled peacefully on our newly acquired tandem up hill and down dale as fields rose and dipped on either side. Sheep momentarily stopped grazing to stare as we went by, and copses rustled, proudly waving their young leaves at us, whilst above, fluffed-up meringue clouds glided lazily in an azure sky.

The passing countryside was now becoming less familiar to me and we seemed a long way from home. We joined the Exeter-bound A-road and the occasional jalopy, motorcyclist, and charabanc, passed us.

"How much further, Dad?" I asked over his shoulder.

"There's a gateway just ahead," Dad said. "We'll pull in there and toss them from the field."

A herd of heifers formed a semi-circle around us, gazing curiously. They hastily shuffled back, eyes rolling, nostrils steaming, as we opened the basket and the pigeons exploded out in a feather-bomb. Up they shot, randomly at first, before forming a group and circling in their usual swoop and dip. I watched as they rapidly became dots before vanishing over the horizon. I was eager now to get home, await their return.

As we eventually trundled the tandem down the lane, my eyes zealously scanned the sky; just empty, cloud-patched deepening blue. Anxiety began to build in me as, having stowed the tandem in Dad's shed, we passed through the garden gate: then joy, oh joy! There they were, perched on their shed roof awaiting their evening meal. "They beat us, Dad, they beat us home." I laughed exultantly. Only later, when I went to feed them, did I realize Father wasn't amongst them. A few days later a letter arrived from Surrey: Father, driven by homing instinct, had returned three hundred miles to his old home. Dad's mate would keep him to race again and send us another cock. Some months later again, another letter arrived to tell us, sadly, Father had been killed by a cat in France whilst returning home from a continental race. He had been identified by his leg ring. Poor Father.

✻ ✻ ✻ ✻ ✻

One day after school there they were! Two oval eggs like bantam eggs, pristine and glistening white. For three weeks I visited morning and evening after school, peeking to see a hen sitting on them. Then finally they hatched; ugly as sin, squirming featherless stubby pink, beaks too big for them and quivering open, demanding food. I watched the hen feeding them as they nudged each other, vying for titbits.

Feathers began to form, and they gradually appeared less ugly as they eyed this new world from their nest. When the hen was absent, I entered the shed and gently lifted one. It was warm and soft, and I could feel its heartbeat, strong and vital. Then one morning they were on the shed floor, squatting and swaying unsteadily as the other pigeons studiously ignored them. But within a few weeks, although still sparsely feathered, they had ventured forth and were soon mingling with the adults. Others were hatched and soon a flock began to build up. We couldn't keep them all, Dad said we'd have to get rid of some; anybody want some pigeons? But the problem was brutally solved when disaster struck. Early one morning Dad returned grim-faced from feeding the chickens. I glanced up from my porridge, wondering what I'd done wrong.

"Rats've got into the pigeon shed overnight," he said, gently.

My heart lurched.

"I'm afraid they've killed some …"

Carnage! I saw feathers and down scattered all around a blood-spattered shed. Bodies lay twisted and gored, some headless, their feet heartbreakingly untouched. Dad had released the four surviving pigeons which now stood on their shed roof, eyeing us, seemingly indifferent to the fate of their companions. Dad threw some grain up to them which they devoured with relish. I could hear the staccato tapping of beaks as, tears misting my eyes, Dad and I removed the mutilated bodies from the shed. We buried them en masse in the small copse at the top of the lane.

Life went on. Others were born, and the flock began to build up again. Soon I was desperately seeking bird-lovers amongst my schoolfriends who might like to adopt a pigeon or two. Pigeons are long livers, but one way or the other, a decade later, our flock had reduced to just two, a cock and a hen. By this time I had long left home to join the navy, and the two remaining pigeons were happily feeding with the chickens.

Then Mum and Dad moved for one last time – and Mum finally had electricity again! It was a newly built bungalow in the railway station village, and the two pigeons were once more confined, this time in a large hutch. Again they were released after a couple of months, and were feeding with the chickens, returning to roost in their hutch at dusk. One day, the hen did not return to feed, nor the next. The cock remained but seemed restless. A few weeks later he, also, failed to return from a flight.

Some months later, on leave one mellow summer's day, I was cycling leisurely along secretive back-lanes of deepest, rustic Devon, when I happened upon a hamlet of a few secluded cottages snuggled shyly in a cleft between steep fields and woodland. A pocket of warm air, piquant with summer scents, lay over the scene, and a brook forded the narrow lane, warbling happily; a swirling mini-galaxy of midges hovered over the water, and the air was vibrant with birdsong.

I espied a flock of several pigeons settled on the thatched roof of one of the cottages. I paused, curious. The colouration was right, and they were a motley bunch. But one pigeon looks much like another. Still, two of them looked almost identical to mine. They gazed insouciantly down at me, perched side by side.

"Hi," I said, and smiled. They blinked enigmatically. "See you've found a new family then." And a serene warmth filled me as I ascended from the dip.

THE OLD RECTORY

The Old Rectory (the name speaks for itself) was part of a manored estate, a large tract of farmland and woodland bordered by the river. The manor house itself stood aloof from Home Farm, the rectory and the estate workers' cottages, the small church (today administered by the parish priest) and its cluster of past workers' graves. It had an extensive walled garden, was secluded and secretive, a good mile from any road and further still from the nearest village. It was little changed from Tudor times. Once, the lord of the manor himself, a grizzled old gentleman with a bushy moustache, rheumy eyes, and clad in country gentleman's clothes from a past decade, trotted past me astride a glossy black mare. Had I observed his approach I would have quickly made myself scarce. As it was, I was trapped; should I touch my forelock and bow my head? Would he look at me, a common serf-child, and lash out with his riding crop for my temerity at impeding his path? In the event, he smiled benignly down upon me, vaguely curious as to my provenance, bade me good morning, and rode on by. His mare, more disdainful than he, arched its head and snorted regally.

Sometimes, helping Dad in the rectory garden, I was dispatched into the woods across the lane to gather leaf mould. It was a sequestered wood of beech and oak, chestnut, and elm; invading rhododendrons and laurel clustered here and there, dense and shining, oddly intimidating. It whispered and rustled upon my entry as if warning of my presence to its denizens and ghosts. Clicks and scuttlings sounded from within the impenetrable depths of the rhododendrons. The sun penetrated the watery gloom only in slender, misted shafts. Sounds of the outside world were muted. Rooks fluttered and quarked high above, woodpigeons flapped panicky away at my approach; song birds were few, their songs ethereal. Sometimes my heart would leap at a sudden harsh screech, and a gaudy-feathered pheasant would scurry away in resentful alarm. Unseen nearby, his dowdy mate would be crouched upon her nest. I would quietly fill my wheelbarrow with leaf mould and slink away.

With the approach of spring, new leaf buds like plump emeralds adorned the trees, rooks began their nest building; deceptively simple structures of twigs in the uppermost branches of the tallest trees. The harsh cadence of their cries would become louder, more vital. They would circle, swoop and bicker, clash briefly over plum nesting sites.

Some weeks later a motley group of men would gather, shotguns under their arms, like casual assassins. They would enter the wood and take up positions beneath the rookery, breech their guns, slip in two cartridges, realign the barrel, raise it to the vertical and blast away in a merciless corvid infanticide. The gentle murmuring of the wood would be shattered by a continuous blast of gunfire, the slaughter persisting for a couple of hours, pellets slashing like angry wasps through the frail twigs and into the soft, warm flesh of fledglings. Many would die, some remain to rot in their nests, maybe to be consumed by their own kind, rooks not being averse to cannibalism, others falling to the feet of their nemesis. But many would survive to nest again next year when the cycle would be repeated. The shooters were not cruel men, but neither were they sentimentalists. Allowed to proliferate uncontrolled, along with woodpigeons, and with no effective natural predators, they would strip the fields bare of seed and crops, devastate a farmer's livelihood. It was all a matter of balance, survival.

On these days Mrs Dutton, reluctant to witness the slaughter, would quietly disappear for the duration.

TREVOR

Tom Baker was a tough old fellow, gnarled and stringy as a war-scarred tomcat, a face weather-beaten and ravaged by seventy years of sun, rain, and biting winds. Pocked by the savage stings of angry wasps which had attacked him when he accidentally hacked into their nest whilst paring a hedge; mean and short-tempered through decades of failed harvests, which he remembered more than the successful ones.

His wife was a little woman, stringy and tough herself, bowed and worn, wrinkled-apple face and age-speckled hands from a lifetime of milking, chicken plucking, rabbit gutting, kitten drowning, and cooking for Tom and their only child, Frank.

Frank in turn was a quiet, gentle child, good-natured but subdued by his repressive and impassioned father, and fettered by owl-like spectacles, and with a large, round, weather-reddened face. But he grew up strong – broad-chested and with powerful arms – proud of the fact that he could shoulder a two-hundredweight sack of potatoes with ease, pitchfork the largest bundle of hay onto the rick or hold a milk churn at arm's length hooked onto his little finger. This however, coupled with Tom's insistence on working the field in the most inclement weather, caused him by middle age to be stricken with arthritis and rheumatism. Only much later, years after Tom's death, when Frank sold the farm and moved to Exeter, did it emerge that he had a head for figures and could hold down a responsible job as a stores' accountant; but all too soon he fell ill and died.

The Bakers lived on Westlake Farm, at the end of a beaten track which led down from Langham Chapel, then continued beyond Westlake to Dennis's Woodtown, becoming more sunken and stony as it went, forded by streams and lined with high hedgerows, where the ghostly whisperings of past farm labourers could sometimes allegedly be heard.

Old Mrs Baker died, leaving Tom and Frank in a fix; the cooking and housework defeated them, so they advertised in *The Western Times* for a housekeeper. And that was when Trevor entered my life: Mrs Kerslake, Trevor's mother and a war widow, became the Baker's housekeeper. She was a warm and passionate woman; exceedingly so, because upon the eventual death of Tom she very soon became Mrs Frank Baker, and along came children on an annual basis, all boys (she was aiming for a football team, she joked, but eventually stopped at eight). Trevor, short, stocky, and with alarmingly blue eyes, possessed, I soon discovered, the same vivid imagination and adventurous spirit as myself. For the rest of my childhood, until the day I said goodbye to all which until then had been my world, crossed the river and left the valley and my childhood behind to join the Royal Navy, we remained the best of friends.

THE RAFT

We'd build a raft, we decided, me and Trevor; we'd read Huckleberry Finn and it all sounded pretty exciting. Well, okay, our river wasn't the Mississippi, not as big, much smaller in fact, no steamboats or whatever, but it still had deep pools, rapids, fish, otters and things, enough water to float a raft. So we'd need materials. Plenty of wood. Binder cord to bind it.

It was the summer holidays. The morning sun came up gold, shimmering bright and full of hope: a good omen. We set off, Micky bounding ahead. We scoured nearby copses and woodlands, collecting fallen and broken branches: not as easy as we had thought: most were too contorted, some rotten. Having selected enough, we relayed them to where a sandbank lay concealed beneath a canopy of riverside oak, aligned them side by side on the sand, and began securing them together with binder cord Trevor had nicked from his father's barn. It was not very successful; they rolled and humped protestingly, cord slithered and snapped and we cursed and sweated.

Eventually, "Tis no use."

We straightened up and looked at each other.

"The cord bain't no use."

"Nor's the wood."

We stood staring at it in morose silence.

"Us need a saw; saw down some trees," Trevor said.

Then, "I know!" I broke into a grin.

"What?"

"Drums – oil drums." I remembered it from a library book I'd read some time ago.

We scoured corners of fields, found a couple of dented oil drums, oil-stained, left them to be collected before sneaking up on farmyards and into barns gloomy with corn dust, thick with chaff and barn owl droppings and infested with rats, but eventually managed to discover four empty oil drums in a tractor shed. Together with the two to be collected it would be enough.

Back on the sandbank, "This cord's useless!"

"You'm right. Wire's what us need."

A pause, brains clicking.

This time it was Trevor. "I know...!"

A stream bounced and fell down a deep gully on its way to the river. An old beech trunk secreted a hornet's nest, and brambles sneaked tentacles across twigs and decomposing leaves. High above the tree canopy a buzzard glided lazily, dive-bombed by indignant rooks. The copse melded smoothly into a grass field, sectioned off only by a disused electric fence, posts sagging, the wire limp between them.

"You reckon the varmer'll miss 'em?"

"T'asn't been used for ages."

We continued disconnecting and looping up the thin, flexible wire.

"If ee do, mind, ee won't know who took un."

"Ee'll guess."

We both laughed a little nervously.

Back on the sandbank we busied ourselves lashing the drums together with the ex-electric wire; under and over, under and over. Finished, we stood back to admire our handiwork.

"Us won't be able to stand on top of 'em like that."

"No, us needs a platform."

Again we looked searchingly at each other. By this time dusk was falling. Conifer tops stood stark against a crimson sunset. Elusive scents rose in a slight mist from the river. Mosquitos danced in a cloud.

"Tomorrow," Trevor said.

"Tomorrow," I agreed.

We left the raft concealed amidst scrub under a riverside elder and went home.

* * * * *

The morrow dawned bright. By nine o'clock we were down on the riverbank, following it along to Baily's marsh where the remains of a fisherman's hut, demolished in a past storm and now just a pile of scattered planks and struts, lay half-buried in the long grass. We selected the best of the planks and struggled back to the raft with them.

The raft groaned and scrunched ominously as we gingerly eased it back onto the sandbank: would it hold together alright?

"Us must tighten the wire," I said.

We placed the planks carefully on top of the drums, secured them with the remaining wire and gazed critically at them. The sun was high now, mosquitos and horseflies beginning to bite, the water sparkling invitingly. A kingfisher flashed past like a sapphire meteor.

"Looks good," I said.

"Yeah, looks good," Trevor agreed.

We hesitated, both nervous of launching it, putting it to the test.

"Must be nigh dinnertime."

Neither of us had watches, not back then.

"Let's launch er after dinner."

"Yeah, let's."

＊ ＊ ＊ ＊ ＊

The sun, past its zenith, was lurking behind a bank of cloud by the time we got back. It was muggy. Micky plunged happily into the water. Our feet were hot in wellingtons. Between us we carefully slid the raft into the river.

"Er's floating!"

Er was, too. She turned sluggishly, began to drift downstream.

"Quick!"

We tried to get a grip, pull ourselves aboard, water pouring into our wellingtons. Once managing it, we tentatively stood upright, the raft rolling precariously until we regained our balance and stood still. Micky, just his head above the water, his long spaniel ears floating either side of it like stabilisers, followed our antics bemusedly as we began drifting slowly, languorously, downstream. Belatedly we realized: no rudder!

"Oh, well, never mind; er'll drift into the bank eventually. We can disembark and make one." I was getting into maritime lingo.

The sun appeared dazzlingly from behind the bank of cloud. Insects blipped on the smooth river surface, a trout jumped, shoals of minnows darted away from us into the sun-dappled shallows. Not the Mississippi maybe, but just as glorious. We had drifted into midstream by now. Seemed to be going a little faster. The surface of the water ahead became ruffled, we could see the pebbled riverbed. A sudden crunching, grating; the raft lurched and we struggled for balance. The planks beneath us began to separate. We could see shifting shale and pebbles now, between detaching oil drums. The front of the raft grounded excruciatingly upon the riverbed, its stern swung around at the same time as the whole structure began to disintegrate and throw us into the water.

As Trevor and I struggled to pull ourselves upright from a foot of water, Micky appeared, prancing beside us, water spraying from his coat, eyes gleaming, barking in high-pitched excitement at this wonderful new game, as the two of us gazed gloomily at the six oil drums rolling and floating haphazardly downstream surrounded by planks and tangled wire.

We stood on the bank, dripping water, gazing at the remains of our raft drifting languidly away; now no more than a pile of debris.

"Bugger that again!" exclaimed Trevor, bitterly. "After all that work!"

"Tell you what," I said, "too many shallows for a raft. Us need something with less displacement." I was pleased at my show of technical nous.

Trevor looked at me.

"A canoe," I said. "Lighter, a shallow draft. Us'll need different materials, tough, and something waterproof."

Trevor's face lit up.

"Buffalo hide. Redskins used buffalo hide! P'raps if us could find a dead cow…!"

But we never did, so lost interest.

WILDCAT

A spring rose in the centre of Brightley lane, bubbled merrily up to trickle down across the tarmacked road at the lane's end, crossing at an angle to be absorbed by the hedgerow, and thence into the field beyond. To the right of the lane was a low hedge anchored by several large beech trees whose canopy extended over the lane to cast a dappled pastel shade of damp gloom, depending upon the weather.

These beeches were the boundary of a tangled woodland which lay steeply over the valley slopes for a mile or more before terminating at Brightley House. Along its craggy length it was infiltrated by precipitous, abandoned quarries, some large, some small, but all rugged and overgrown by scrub and saplings. Slate, blue and thinly layered, with the occasional large granite boulder protruding dominantly through it, constituted the jagged, canting escarpments and precipices. Here and there, shelves of stony soil sloped gently back to high, impending elevations of smooth, shiny slate, at the base of which lay small and gloomy cavities. Woodland lay at the tops of these quarries; oak, beech and holly grew here, many stunted and misshapen by the wild elements that swept across the valley. Between these trees, concealed amidst fern and bramble, were mysterious hollows, some quite deep and with miniature grottos at their rear, in which dwelt fairies and wood elves. At least, in mine and Trevor's opinions they did; a flash of muted emerald, a splash of red, a tiny, flitting something...

Few humans ventured into this steep and oblique woodland. It was the province of wild things – shy, secretive, some predatory, others timid, small and wary troglodytes – a region of resonance, rustlings, twitterings and snorts, squeaks and grunts which abruptly hushed into watchful hesitation, and intrusive and intrinsic silence, should a curious human pass by, then mount again like a rewound gramophone when the intruder had passed.

The trees grew quite close-packed in places, abundant with chirps and whistles, a twitching and shuddering of leaves, unseen denizens living out their arboreal lives, hunting, mating, oblivious to and uncaring of any wider world. Peer between the tree boles and one could see, way below, the serpentine river glinting silver between its ragged banks, green fields dotted with sheep, rush-invaded marshland, a solitary gamekeeper's cottage peeking through trees on the far skyline.

To the left of the road which swung past Gwen's white stone at the entrance to Brightley Drive, the largest, highest quarry virtually bisected the woodland. Gorse, vivid, gay yellow in spring, climbed its flanks, from which slatey scree gave way to large boulders and sheer slate walls, the highest of which rose sheer to the severed woodland on the right. Rabbits lived and bred freely amidst the gorse, lizards sun-bathed on warm slate, and jackdaws, querulous and harshly rowdy, constructed their nests, inaccessible to predators, in deep clefts in the slate walls and between boulders.

One humid summer's day, Trevor and I climbed this quarry, Micky too; mountain men, outlaws, scree and dust slithering beneath our scrabbling feet until we reached a narrow and precipitous trail running directly beneath two large boulders. These loomed threateningly over us before we clambered up a steep, earthy slope at their edge to the summit of the quarry. From here, having outwitted the posse, we paused to gaze up the valley where the mauve-misted crags of Dartmoor lay hazed in the far distance, before turning into the woods. Here, a dappled, shady softness embraced us. We could sense the sudden hush, hidden eyes fixed warily upon us, feel the carpet of damp leaf mould beneath our feet as we advanced cautiously over the woodland floor.

After a few paces along the sloping ground and using moss-covered boles of trees for support, we approached the crumbly, uneven lip of a quarry. Squinting in the suddenly unimpeded sunlight, we gazed over a sheer drop of a hundred and thirty feet or so to a wide ledge below. Beyond this, a green, tangled jungle tumbled riotously down to the narrow ribbon of Brightley Drive before dropping still further to the riverbank, where the water gleamed and sparkled under the sun like a trillion shooting stars.

Using tree trunks as handholds, we skirted the quarry, stumbling and slithering gleefully around its outer rim; slipping, laughing, bouncing on our derrières, struggling upright only to tumble again until we eventually swung onto the forest floor and stumbled upright. Beneath our feet stunted grass and tiny, light-blue violets basked amidst groundsel and nettles, which sprouted and flourished between shards and slivers of broken slate and warm, crumbly soil. A heat haze shimmered over them and moist, oppressive heat bore down upon us like a damp blanket. Midges roiled in a misty cloud; bees, flies and woodwasps buzzed and hummed. A snake, silver-sheened and sunning itself on a smooth slab of slate, sensed our presence and corkscrewed sinuously away before we could identify it. A red admiral butterfly edged its explorative way around a nettle leaf. We watched it shimmer away before turning to look up the crenulated face of the quarry.

Scrub, ash saplings and tree roots protruded here and there. Rocks, some large, thrust determinedly from aeons past when a tropical ocean covered the land, intimations of which were brought home to us by Trevor's sudden exclamation.

"Look!" He was bent over a large rock protruding from the ground at the face's foot. "A fossil!" And it seemed so; not common in our area, but unmistakable: the clear imprint on the rock of a large, half-moon shell shape through which arced vaulted lines decreasing in length to its base. I ran my fingers gently over the indented shape as a tremor of awe at the incomprehensible aeons of past time shivered through me. I tried to pick up the rock, but, like an iceberg, it was only the tip of a much larger, subterranean one.

Meanwhile, Trevor was gazing up at the quarry face.

"I reckon us could climb that," he said.

I looked dubious.

"If hill-billies wi' huntin' dogs wuz after us, us could," he said.

I gazed to the edge of the quarry face. Noted the various handholds and footholds: it was possible.

"I kin yur the dogs!" exclaimed Trevor, beginning to climb.

Carefully, diligently, we began the ascent, using clefts and crannies, grasping protesting saplings for leverage.

Crumbly soil and slivers of slate trickled from under our feet. I began to sweat. Once, I slipped, grabbed a sapling which strained ominously at its roots before I managed to stabilise myself. Although well to the side of the sheer face, the climb was sharply steep, almost vertical in places. There were overhanging trees and scrub only a few feet to our left as we slowly eased our way towards the top.

That's when I saw it. My eyes widened; I froze, one foot high above the other, one hand clasping a protruding tree root.

It was lying crouched along the limb of an overhanging oak, long legs splayed in front of it, paws pulsing softly, claws sinking effortlessly into the bark. The long, sinuous body exuded power, menace, had light tabby stripes; a chimera which appeared to blend amorphously with leaf-shadow. Only its head seemed distinct, solid and feral with long side whiskers. These lifted like gossamer abreast a snarling mouth displaying fangs of gleaming ivory and above which two large orbs blazed in green malevolence. Before I recovered enough to tell Trevor, it had gone; utterly silent, dissolved chameleon-like into the trees.

"A wanderin' farm cat," Trevor, clinging to a groaning sapling nearby, opined.

But he hadn't seen it. I know what I saw, and it was no farm cat, no domestic puss, but a creature which exuded a savage power, a fearful beauty, a virulent demi-god of the wildwood; in short, a wildcat. In a momentary epiphany it was revealed to me many hidden things; from the numerous varieties of insects creeping, scuttling on the forest floor, to the submarine waterlife of the river, the burrowing subterranean life, the larger mammals, all secretive and expertly evasive and barely even on the periphery of human awareness. And wildcats, thought long extinct in England, the most perspicaciously evasive of all.

But who would believe me?

THE RIVER

On clear days purple moorland could be seen brooding on the far horizon. From it, a patchwork of fields and woodlands emerged from a blue mist to sweep and tumble closer and closer until it merged seamlessly with our valley. And with it came the river which ran through the seasons of our childhood. The river rose near the coast in North Devon, flowed in a vast loop encompassing a substantial area of the county, contorting and winding until joining the sea within a few miles of its source. Our valley was one small loop, within the larger loop, and contained sparsely populated farmland dotted by farmhouses and cottages, knolls and dips and small remaining sections of wildwood, still secretive and seldom visited by humans, dark and tangled and permeated by sly creaks, whisperings and fleeting shadows.

The river ran through this landscape like a separate living entity, its voice mingling harmoniously with the passing wind. Only on approach to its banks did it become more distinctive, a timeless rippling rush transporting damp river-scent exclusive to itself and carried on misted spray and air-cooled water flowing smooth over submerged rocks, slate outcrops, and time-smoothed pebbles.

River life teemed, ranging from tiny larvae clamped stoically to the underside of pebbles, through to freshwater shrimps, river mussels, loaches, and miller's thumb fish to brown trout, and great salmon returning from vast and icy Arctic waters to the river of their birth. Eels too, tiny elvers all the way from their birthplace in the Sargasso Sea. Otters hunted the salmon and men with dogs hunted the otters. Grey herons left their rickety nests high in elm and ash to flap like fallen clouds up-stream, where they stood silent and long-legged, cruel-eyed and poised to pierce unwary fish with yellow razor-sharp beaks. Riverside trees cast dappled light over tranquil pools, creating rippling water-pictures where fallen leaves cruised in aimless circles.

Summer, and we children crossed sun-baked meadows to sandy, tree-shaded spurs where sand martins swooped with perfect aim into nests deep in sandy river banks and where grey wagtails bobbed and kingfishers flashed in blue fire.

We stripped and swam and lifted pebbles to watch loaches and bullheads arrow zig-zag away and sunbeams bounce off the water like golden bullets. A salmon leapt, arced high in a rainbow of spray which brushed our faces with a touch of the river goddess. Warily, we approached shaded pools, sinisterly quiescent, brooding and silent and funeral-black, where amorphous shapes glided below the surface from which we backed cautiously away.

Cattle came to drink, their great heads bowing to the water, snorting contentedly, hooves crackling over the pebbles and muddying the stream, depositing cowpats which attracted excited horse flies.

* * * * *

Each school holiday Trevor and I explored a little further upstream where we discovered lush meadows, reed-shrouded marshes, and a long-abandoned orchard, forgotten now. There, in spring, sheets of pink and white apple blossom spread in a nimbus cloud over trees fallen and decaying amidst brambles and bracken. We discovered sun-dappled islands bridged by fallen trees across which we scrambled to discover shaded arbours of bluebells and primroses, periwinkles, and wood-anemones. Spiders scuttled shyly, earwigs and beetles fussed around fallen, decaying boughs. Empty river-mussel shells left by feasting herons glinted mother-of-pearl in the rich undergrowth. A river-breeze washed over the islands and we breathed deeply of its cool fragrance, closing our eyes to hear only the whisper of the trees, the song of the river as we stood captive in an enchanted land known only to us.

* * * * *

On autumn evenings of a full moon we liked to walk the river banks, watch the ethereal mist rise, and listen to the silvery laughter of water over burnished pebbles. Fields lay silent under the twilight air, grass hummocks became fairy tale, gem-encrusted castles. With approaching night the valley slopes acquired purple hollows and dark veiled caves. Distant oil lamps came on, specks of reassuring gold in the lengthening shadows, and across the river scarlet dust from a drowned sun hung suspended above darkened, cascading forest. A barn owl soared low and soundlessly over the meadow, spectral in the velvet dusk. The deep ocean of night now beckoned: islands of stars, impossibly distant.

One enchanted crystalline night we watched a full moon rise, felt the world hold its breath. Huge and fiery-red at first, turning smudged silver, it climbed into the sky, scattering moon-dust all around. It was king now, lavishing the world with its bounty. A moon-breeze whispered transparent fingers through a riverside elder, its clusters of wine-ripe fruit shimmered crimson and its gnarled branches swayed and creaked worshipfully. The breeze fluttered across the river to oscillate threads of silver like vibrating harp-strings. It lifted the elusive fragrance of willowy balsam, carried it into the night, and we thought we were breathing moon-scent.

Late one autumn a great wind came in the night. Far out over the Atlantic it gathered pace and strength, slammed its way over the moor, grounding skylarks and stonechats, sending polecats to seek shelter in the nearest available burrow, howled maliciously down the head of our valley and crashed through its wooded slopes in a tsunami of sound.

I awoke to hear an angry demon battering at my window, heard snaps and cracks and thumps of tumbling objects in the garden, rolling tin can sounds, and with it came the rain in furious, staccato attack, attempting to drill holes in the windowpane. It rammed its way under the overhang of thatch in a discordant drumroll as I lay fearfully under the blankets, listening. In my vivid imagination it was some huge beast tormented by pain and issuing mournful sighs and anguished wails.

Eventually I drifted off to sleep, tormented by dreams of wounded dragons in fatal conflict with white knights.

By dawn it had abated, rampaged eastwards, leaving behind a twitchy, neurotic breeze.

"A couple've apple trees are down," Dad said, over breakfast, "and half the blinkin' roof's off the chicken shed. God knows what else!"

Later, Trevor and I walked the banks of the swollen river gazing in awe at up-rooted trees grinding downstream, turning and gyrating in the water, groaning as they clashed against the bank. One had jammed itself lengthways across the arches of the bridge, muddy water gushing under and over it, quivering its leafless branches like the legs of a nightmare, dying insect.

Further upstream a large oak was down, bridging the brook, and we edged across it, laughing and adventurous, using its now vertical branches as handholds. Micky followed, balancing like a circus dog.

The storm, we heard later, had claimed the lives of a number of cattle, sheep and horses.

Soon after, the rains came in force and a uniform greyness descended upon the land. All day, shadows lingered along the valley slopes and the river turned brown, turgid with displaced earth. Farmers eyed it warily and herded their livestock to higher ground.

Briefly the rain eased to a furry drizzle. Crossing a field, the ground sucked at our feet like a possessive lover. In the woods, trees shed water-bombs which detonated icy trickles under our collars and down our spines. Then, come evening and after dark, we heard it; gentle at first, almost timid, tickling the windowpanes, and we paid it no attention. I sat in the lamplight reading a comic, Valerie was on the floor with her dolls and Mum was busy in the kitchen. Dad came home from work, shook rain from his mac and cap, hanging them on a peg behind the door.

"Just made it, I think," he remarked. "It's getting heavier. Are the chickens shut in?"

"I've done it, Dad." I glanced up from Wilson of *The Wizard*.

"Good lad."

We could hear it louder now against the glass.

"Is that it, Eed?" Dad scowled at the supper before him. "Not much for a working man."

"There's more potatoes," said Mum, vaguely defensive. "More cabbage. More bread – there's bread. That meat's got to last for tomorrow."

"Gosh, listen to that!" I exclaimed.

We all glanced up at the window. It was gunning now, a constant, hissing roar, cascading down the windowpanes.

"Ground's already saturated," said Dad. "Much more of this'n the river'll be over…"

Little rivulets were trickling under the door, vacillating ripples picking up grains of earth from Dad's discarded boots.

"I'll get the mop," said Mum. "Some old towelling or something to block it."

"I hope Mick's alright," I said, suddenly anxious.

"He'll be okay," said Dad. "His kennel's sturdy. Anyway, we can't open the door or we'll be flooded! It'll ease up in a minute; it can't keep this up."

But it could. It was still persisting when I went to bed an hour later. I peered anxiously from my bedroom window, from where I could just distinguish Micky's kennel below. Rain streamed in a waterfall from its transverse roof, flowed around and under its base. He would be dry inside, though, on his straw bed, I comforted myself. Even so, I lay awake worrying until it eventually eased to a steady patter. And now I could hear the river, an angry roar, a deep undertone which made me uneasy.

While I slept the river breached its banks. It lapped stealthily across the meadows with baleful intent, routing numerous insects from the grass, sending water-voles scurrying in its vanguard. Reaching the hedgerows, it slurped lasciviously, creeping higher to slither lymphatic fingers into rabbit warrens, panicking the inhabitants into dashing for escape burrows on higher ground. There were many deaths that night, quiet and plaintive; moles, shrews, and voles unaware in their subterranean dens until it was too late, a couple of predatory weasels trapped in a mole run, several stray sheep, and a cow and her new-born calf missed by a careless farmer.

I awoke to see the sun shining through my window, a polished blue sky. I could hear Micky shuffling around in his kennel, a deep roar registering and I remembered. I slipped from my bed and opened the window. Puddles lay around Micky's kennel and on the cement patch outside our front door. The garden scowled dankly brown, sorry for itself. But it was the transformed valley below that fascinated me; the familiar meadows and hedges had vanished, replaced by a great lake rippling silver under the sun. Dazzling pearls danced playfully across it, hedge-top trees protruding from it like broken masts of sunken galleons. And beyond the lake a great beast writhed and twisted, roaring savagely; our river, no longer friendly, but terrifying, and I was instantly relieved that our cottage lay high up the hillside.

* * * * *

By the weekend the waters had receded back into the river, brown and turgid, bucking and swirling violently, seemingly angry at again being contained after its brief bid for freedom. On Saturday morning,

Valerie and I walked down to the lower meadow with Micky. Grass, sorrel and thistles lay flattened, beaten and exhausted by the waters. Scattered puddles glinted placidly in the sunlight. A few yards away we could hear the river growling bearishly just a few inches below its banks.

"Look!" exclaimed Valerie. "Over there."

"What?"

"In that big puddle; something moved."

There was something there alright, I could see it arrowing, creating a bow wave.

We headed excitedly towards it. Beneath our wellingtons the saturated meadow groaned and squeaked. We hesitated as we neared the puddle, half afraid.

"It won't jump out at us, will it?" wondered Valerie.

"Go for our throats, perhaps," I suggested.

Valerie halted abruptly. "You don't think so, do ee?"

"No, daft maid: look, tis a fish."

"Oh … the poor thing's trapped."

"Marooned," I said.

We approached it warily. It was big. It stopped thrashing, lay dormant, we could see its mouth gasping, its gills opening and closing. A fish eye gazed coldly at us. Micky edged towards it, gave it a wary sniff from a foot away and decided it wasn't his sort of prey, so headed back to the intriguing scents of the hedgerow.

"It's a salmon," I said. "We could take it home, have it for dinner. Dad would be pleased with us."

Valerie looked dubious. "Seems a shame," she said.

"Git away!" I said.

The salmon thrashed again, weaker now, half out of the water. Its gaze seemed fixed defiantly upon us.

I looked around. "I need something to knock it on the head with," I said. "A stone or something."

"Maybe," said Valerie, "we could just lift it, put it back in the river, save its life."

"Yes, but…"

"I don't like to kill it; it seems sad."

We gazed unspeaking at it for a while. Seeing it there helpless, looking at us, I didn't either.

It took us a while. We were heedful to keep our hands away from its mouth. Every time I got a grip it slithered from my grasp. I was surprised at its strength. The puddle was slowly being absorbed into the earth, leaving the salmon more and more exposed to the air. Its struggles became weaker and finally, between us, we managed to get our hands under it and lift it from the diminishing puddle. It struggled feebly and once got free to lie flapping helplessly upon the grass, gasping, gazing inscrutably up at us.

Eventually we neared the river with it, wary now; not of the salmon but the river, which roared so loud we had to shout to be heard above it. We could see it rolling and tumbling frighteningly, forming transient whirlpools no more than a foot below the bank. Slowly we eased forward until we could feel spray upon our faces.

"That's far enough," I said. "I'll count to three, right? On three, throw it as hard as you can."

"… Three!"

Its tail just clipped the bank, taking a clod of earth with it as it plummeted, instantly swallowed by the muddied waters.

"There," grinned Valerie, "our good deed for the day. Oh! Look." Her grin vanished abruptly.

Swirling in the current at the centre of the river was what I at first thought to be a large blob of dirty froth, then realized it was a sheep.

"It's not alive, is it?" exclaimed Valerie, shocked.

"No." It was dead. You could tell. It slowly rolled over as we watched, four hooved legs pointing stiffly at the sky. I briefly saw its head before it re-submerged. We watched it in sombre silence until it was swept from our view, then headed solemnly back across the meadow.

It rained again that night. From my bedroom window next morning I could glimpse the re-invigorated river writhing and bucking like a mythical water-snake; a gigantic earthworm broken free from the bowels of the world, taunting us by licking again at its constraining banks.

But the rain had passed and the battling sun thrust aside wrathful clouds with shards of brilliant light, which danced over water and meadow and emerald woodland, and a gentle rainbow arced over the land. We squinted into its jewelled arch, seeking its end to which we set forth with spade and trowel to dig for the pot of gold. But rainbows possess mischievous spirits, shifting wonders which transmute and shyly dissolve when approached, so we veered off to explore the nearby wildwood instead.

Next day, like a shamed and violent drunk now sober, the river shushed its tamed and migratory waters, bidding them farewell on their eternal journey to the sea.

ARCHIE'S WHEEL

England is a highly populated country (by humans, that is) but there are still (thank goodness) areas sparsely populated: indeed, where humans seldom venture. Woodlands, briar-tangled and canting wildly and, for city folk, inhabited by half-imagined creatures which sting and bite; poisonous reptiles waiting to pounce, poisonous plants waiting to seduce with colourful, attractive berries or flowers; maybe even the legendary Green Man. There are brooding moorlands harbouring lethal bogs and high granite, shadow-swept tors beneath which witches' covens (composed of feral double-life city folk) offer sacrifices and indulge in obscene rituals under a full moon. Oh yes. But enough, you get the gist.

In our valley, an oblong of approximately 24 miles by 12, sandwiched between the A386 and the A3124 and intersected only by the B3217, lay thirty or so square miles of rolling farmland and woodlands thinly spidered by veins of dung- and mud-spattered, single-track country roads with stony, untarmacked lanes leading to isolated farms and thatched, ancient cottages. Clusters of small villages and tiny hamlets lay sparsely scattered, randomly evolved from Anglo-Saxon times.

From the hilltop chapel, a single-track road angles down between antiquated hedgerows to the bridge over the Torridge, before rising again a mile or so to the A386. A few yards down from the chapel, this single-track road declines away a couple of miles, growing steeper and craggier and dotted by raggle-taggle copses as it goes, until reaching a U-bend of the river. Dolton Mill and the tumbled ruins of what was once a small building for dyeing cloth, later a dwelling house, were the only buildings to the west of the Dolton settlements.

Directly behind this ruin, and now encroaching upon it, lies a corner of Halsdon Cover (woods). The cover climbs steeply, to where a lofty stand of mature beech trees defies the elements on a high ridge, before falling even more steeply to a track immediately paralleling the river. This was one of mine and Trevor's favourite spots. Wending our way up from the vaguely spooky ruins, we clambered along rims of long-abandoned quarries and sheer-sided gullies, higher and higher through ragged clusters of closely matted rhododendrons, and a half-buried line of slate debris seemingly once a wall – a tantalizing suggestion of time-absorbed conformity run wild – until reaching these majestic, windswept beeches from which we could glimpse, far below, patches of silver-glinting river. A large flat field bordering a fir forest rose high and regal on the other side.

Initials were carved into most of the beeches, some so expanded by the tree's growth they were like old, untreated scars, barely decipherable. Others less so, but all time-honoured. We added ours to them with our penknives, Micky's too, whilst wondering as to the former's antecedence. We hunted around for large stones or small boulders half buried under leaf mould at the base of trees. These we set rolling, underarm for momentum, watching, thrilled, as their speed increased, faster and faster, bouncing agilely, violently, from dips, cannoning off trees, gaining speed and strength. Some reached the bottom of the slope with a thrilling velocity, hurtling over the track like lethal missiles, which indeed they would have been were anyone strolling unawares along the path, before plunging into the river with the force of a falling meteorite. More often than not however, they were abruptly halted in their progress by slamming, juddering, against the bole of a mature tree.

✳ ✳ ✳ ✳ ✳

We spotted it half-concealed by summer growth on the inside of the hedge bordering the road with Archie Parkhouse's field. A young ash grew atop the hedge casting formless shadows over it, flickering across the rust-smeared steel band on its rim from which dulled wooden spokes angled symmetrically to its central hub. Once, it had ground, crunching, over stony lanes, churned ruts into tarmacked road, sludged through farmyard mud, left its trail in soft cornfield soil as the summer sun struck hot from the moulded steel. Back then it had been attached to a horse-drawn cart collecting corn sheaves of dusty gold. It had carted mud-splattered turnips and mangolds from winter fields to barn storage, rumbled leisurely, piled high with hay, over fields shimmering under a warm June sun.

It could have been a hundred years old, finally made redundant by the new-fangled tractor. Whatever. Somehow, it had become disconnected from its cart and lain carelessly to rest in the chromatic, pastel-washed tumult of grass and flora thriving beneath the proud young ash.

Until, that is, Trevor and I happened across it.

Which of us thought of it first, I've forgotten. Either way, it was an exciting prospect; the thought of it crashing crazily down through the woods at incredible speed, like a rampaging, skyborne chariot.

It was heavy and as tall as us. We lugged it upright, leaving its imprint in the hedge, and, laughing excitedly, rolled it across the field. A couple of times we lost its balance, leaping nimbly aside to avoid broken bones as it thumped dolefully to the ground. But eventually we manoeuvred it through a gate into the adjoining field, which sloped gently down to a farm lane. Thence another field, scattered with ragwort, docks and thistles, and which canted sharply down to the bed of the valley. Here, we let it roll freely, watched gleefully as it wobbled, gaining speed and momentum before barging into the weed-strewn, boggy base of the field. It vacillated, quivered, before toppling into the mud. Running, leaping in its wake, we waded, mud sticking to our wellingtons, towards it. We watched it settle into brown-black mud, rising air bubbles popping between the spokes.

"Quick, don't let un sink!"

We reached down, hands in the mud under its rim, and struggled to lift it upright. It was an effort. It slipped a couple of times, and we quickly grabbed it before it began to sink again. By now we were liberally splattered from the neck down by gaseous-smelling mud. Unable to upright it, we dragged it, heaving, panting, and cursing, towards the brook which separated the field from Halsdon Wood. Here we paused, standing in clear, shallow water at the edge of the singing brook. Above us, sunlight rippled shadowy through the trees to strike halfway up the field in a line dividing gloom from bright, leaving us in a dismal half-light. Birdsong echoed from the woods, contrasting with the drear plop and slurp of escaping foul air from the bog to which Trevor now pointed.

"Look."

It looked at first like a large, slime-covered rock, a disparate shape rising from the mud, until I spotted the dulled, crusted horns, a skull half-sunken. Mosquitoes swarmed over it in a cloud, a couple of blowflies. Conversely, a brilliant, steely-azure dragonfly circled concentrically. The carcass was hairless, hide no longer leather but revoltingly, smoothly slimy.

"Been there a long time," I said. Died there, sucked slowly down? Or dumped by some farmer to avoid the cost of legal removal? We could only guess.

We turned, grabbed up the wheel and trundled it across the brook, crystal water dripping from it as we manoeuvred it falteringly through a gap in the sunken elder- and hazel-strewn hedge before setting off in stages up through the wood.

It was a long and strenuous haul, a struggle for it not to slip back. Every few moments we lowered it flat, sweating profusely, laughing self-deprecatingly at the stupidity of what we were doing, before we inched our way painstakingly higher.

Eventually, amazingly, stubbornly, we reached the summit and flopped exhausted down by the beeches, the wheel beside us.

We rested awhile, not talking, lying flat on our backs. Above us, verdant leaves filtered sunlight to cast a flux of soft shade over us. A warm breeze blew, and for a moment I thought I could smell a salt-encrusted, distant ocean, cool cerulean rollers, and palm-shaded islands. A mewl made me open my eyes to see a buzzard, high overhead, riding a thermal current. Several rooks, black shards of night, were, as ever, dive-bombing it then veering sharply away. The buzzard ignored them.

I sat up. Blinked rapidly several times, refocusing my eyes. I could hear the breeze soft in the trees, the steady rush of the river far below, while beyond it, across the flat grassfield, the fir forest floated in a dusty haze.

"Right, let's get er rollin'!" I scrambled to my feet. Between us we lugged the wheel upright, nigh as tall as us, steadied it. We paused briefly, seeking the clearest route through the trees. Silent awhile; Wild West settlers tensely awaiting the signal.

"Let er roll!"

And off er went, with the aid of a vigorous push from us. Slow at first, unsteady. The hub nicked the side of a tree, leaving a white scar, and we held our breath thinking she would topple. But no.

Gaining speed now, jumping a little on the uneven gradient. Faster. The hub cracked against another tree, spinning her off course, but another set her back again. Speeding now, twigs and dead leaves spurting wildly from the steel rim, unstoppable, saplings whiplashing viciously aside.

We stood frozen in awe, vaguely uneasy at the havoc we had set in motion. The fury of protesting sound in its flight was frightening.

Then: abrupt silence.

The wheel had reached the lip of the forest above the path at breath-taking velocity, spokes a blur, sunlight rebounding from the steel rim. It took off, airborne high over the path, bounced once, a dull thunk on the riverbank, a fulcrum to send it high again before descending toward the river. A roiling white pillar of water shot from the placid surface sending frantic ripples to break like surf over the hump of a pebble bank. The pillar fountained gracefully back on itself. The ruffled surface slowly settled.

There was no sign of the wheel.

"Cor!" We laughed wildly, jumped up and down. "Did ee ever ...? What'd ee reckon?"

* * * * *

Shadow was deepening, climbing higher up the field opposite, as we strutted gleefully back through the wood. Micky was rousting something from deep amidst a riot of feral rhododendrons. The sombre ruin below us crouched in deep shade, its jagged cob chimneystack reaching like a beckoning witch's finger.

I shuddered.

* * * * *

Safe at home. *Children's Hour, The Wizard* comic, boiled egg then bread and jam for tea. A falling night, evening scents drifting through the open door, an owl's cry, a fox's scream, a flitting bat; tranquil light from our oil lamp keeping ghost and ghouls at bay.

A wave of undiluted happiness at the end of a perfect day of adventure.

* * * * *

"Twas you two divels, I know twas," scolded Archie. His eyes gleamed playfully in the leathery, tanned face, stubby pipe clamped between his teeth; the sweet, homely smell of tobacco.

"Not us, Archie," we said.

We had inadvertently encountered him and his aging docile pony along the valley road, some days later.

But he knew that we knew that he … well, you know.

DOLTON VALLEY

It was a strangely isolated place which the villagers knew simply as The Valley. Wooded hills climbed high on either side and the sun rose late and set early. We children traversed the valley on the way home from school, descending narrow, tarmacked West Lane hemmed in by high hedgerows. Pastures and woodlands, ever unknown to us, rolled away into bleak hills and shaded vales. Dark and tangled woodlands harboured shy and secretive beasts, and low-lying bogs muttered and plopped, gaseously ingesting the odd sheep or cow unfortunate enough to have wandered beyond the safety of its pasture.

Tiny rills trickled and wound through this landscape, cutting and creating arteries which eventually joined a brook forging its serpentine route to the river. This brook briefly appeared, shallow and translucent and rippling musically over time-worn pebbles, to be spanned by a low wooden bridge bordering the lane. Here we paused on balmy sun-soaked summer afternoons, lingered awhile, cast sticks, sat on the rail-less bridge, and dangled our feet in the cooling water.

It was a quiet, peaceful spot at a bend in the lane. Rich birdsong like discordant crystal bells emerged from a wood across the lane. A buzzard soared high above and the trees were dense in deep shadow, which seemed to whisper seductively intimidating, and we dared not enter. Instead, we removed our shoes and socks and paddled downstream between sandy banks and green-dappled shade until the water became too deep and the shade opaque. Scrub greedily overhung the banks and, in dim disarray behind it, shrubs and ferns breathed a silky caution as the brook veered away from the road.

Again, now in the lowest point of the valley, the brook appeared weaving shyly, bubbling and spuming beneath elder, hazel and willow. Eels could be spotted in the deeper pools, sinuous dark shapes shadowy beneath the undercut banks and gritty bed, creating mud-clouds of decomposing leaves and twigs. In winter, with leafless trees, it became more visible, grey, and matted silver, and after heavy rain, angry, growling, and turgid brown, threatening to burst its banks and overlap the neighbouring fields from which grazing livestock would be hastily evacuated. In January, clusters of snowdrops like burnished pearls bobbed gaily in an icy breeze, a white green-tinted garland embracing the brook, harbingers of coming spring with the brook again hidden behind a blanket of viridescence.

A clutch of dwellings, some with faded whitewash, a couple unplastered and exposing bare cob, canting wearily, battered by the elements of centuries, lay scattered in the base of the valley as if having sprouted there naturally like hill-side fungi. Autumn mists rising from the brook would close in upon them, clinging wraiths rendering them insubstantial blurred ghosts from an earlier time, as perhaps they were; homes to weary bucolics, their spirits now just inherent whispers in the mist, resonant in the hoot of an owl, the mewl of a buzzard; resentful of our now less pain-wreaked, easier, and longer lives.

Resident there in my time was a diverse assemblage of characters, colourful and not a little eccentric. Archie Parkhouse, smallholder. His hillside fields too steep for cultivation, he bred a few sheep, kept a milking cow for his own use. Chickens roamed freely. Geese and ducks; some Muscovy and tufted ducks mingled freely with the more common mallards, all of which splashed and swam happily in the transient waters of the brook. Archie was also the local pig slaughterer and rabbit trapper. We children on our way home from school would sometimes meet him, and his aging pony pulling its creaking trap whereupon evil-toothed gin traps swayed alongside their furry victims suspended heads down, unseeing death-glazed eyes and blood-caked nostrils, performing a dance macabre upon the jigging trap.

"Ow be ee, Archie?" we would say, standing close to the hedge as he passed.

And Archie would smile amiably, a stubby tobacco pipe clasped between his teeth, lift a hand in acknowledgement; for despite his livelihood, Archie was not a cruel man, but a man versed in his trade, raised a countryman essential to his time, unsentimental, non-anthropomorphic. A life outdoors had creased his features like tanned leather, hewn his hands gnarled and roughened by toil. He wore a battered and stained trilby above a face eagle-eyed and starkly handsome. His keen eyes sparkled mischievously. He had a reclusive wife only seen when feeding the chickens and ducks, the possessor of a melancholy mien and Norfolk accent seldom heard in more than a brief sentence. There were no children to the best of my knowledge.

Archie's house looked down upon the lane and above the flood level of the brook. At its rear a dry-stone wall held at bay a tumbling grass field, beyond the near horizon of which lay climbing fields and veiled copses and, way above, two farms, Woodtown and Westlake, homes to Dennis and Trevor respectively.

A long ramshackle shed of time-warped planks and rusting corrugated galvanized sheets flanked the road by his yard, and we would peer curiously, a little warily, into its depths where spidery dark shadows seemed to flit around an antiquated hay wain listing amidst rusting farm implements, pitchforks, and mysteriously archaic artefacts. Gin traps, brown-stained with ancient blood, hung jumbled on cobwebby walls. A smell of dust and yesteryear hung over all.

Some years later, as an adult, I came across Archie leaning over a gate of a field, puffing his pipe, and gazing fondly at his pony which was contentedly munching hay.

"Good Lord, Arch, you still got him? He must be ancient!" I said.

"Aye, ee be that, bay, sure nuff." He smiled at me. "Thirty, or there 'bouts, I reckon."

Down in the valley things were much the same. Ducks still preened, waddled and swam. Geese honked and hissed, lowered their heads threateningly at strangers. But the dogs were gone and the shed was slowly collapsing in on itself and the contents.

Years later, Trevor informed me that Archie had died. "Cancer. I went to see un een 'ospital. Wished I 'adn't. Didn't recognize un at all. All haggard'n shrunk, ee wuz; not Archie at all. Just a shell. Yeah, wished I 'adn't gone."

* * * * *

Next door to Archie's stood the Phillips brothers' cottage facing the lane from above a high bank, plaster muddied-white and bulging in places, crumbling here and there to reveal grey-yellow patches of cob. The windows were impenetrable, leaning back in their frames to reflect the sky as if fearing a fall over the bank and into the brook below. The brothers themselves we rarely saw; reclusive, only occasionally spotted, blue-overalled and toiling in the distance of a field. Once or twice we might see them outside their cottage and offer a timid hello, receiving a quiet, succinctly polite acknowledgement.

One day an ambulance stood outside, blocking the lane, and we inched around it, curious and a little awed (never having seen one before), trying to peer into its dim interior. A disinfectant smell of mortality. Two attendants emerged, inching their way through the cottage door, holding a stretcher between them. A covered mound lay upon it, a pale, indistinct face, unmoving. We watched them manoeuvre it into the ambulance before closing the doors and driving away.

"Do ee reckon ee's daid?" asked Trevor.

The sepulchral odour of disinfectant still lingered.

"Dunno. Probably dyin', anyway." A further queasiness of the stomach.

He didn't die, because we glimpsed them both again a few weeks later, paring the hedge beyond the brook.

"Couldn'a been that bad, then," I said, vaguely disappointed. The others solemnly agreed.

* * * * *

A few minutes later we stoned a viper to death. It was inoffensively sunning itself on the deserted road and all vipers had to be killed because they were poisonous. Such was our way of ignorant thinking.

It wasn't a viper, anyway, not even a snake, but a harmless slow-worm, a legless lizard. I felt guilt afterwards every time we passed the spot where its body, sheen gone, dulling silver, lay flat and embedded in the tarmac. Such is the casual cruelty of children.

A few years later, having left school and obtained a job labouring on a farm, I came across one of the Phillips brothers paring a hedge along Langham Road. He paused and smiled amiably at me. He knew my name and I wondered how.

"I yur you'm joinin' the navy," he said, his voice gentle, accent pronounced but diction explicit. He went on to tell me he had been a sergeant in the army. "Some yurs ago now, mind." Had travelled the world. How then, had he ended up living with his brother in a lowly cottage in a hidden combe in deepest Devon? I didn't ask. Had he never married? Again I didn't ask. I had always imagined the brothers, like Archie and most other rustics, had spent their whole lives within a few miles of the area.

Bob Brown lived next door to the Phillips brothers. Grey was his colour: grey hair, grey moustache, worn-grey clothes, and grey sullen demeanour. The only thing not grey was his wooden leg. He had lost the original in the Great War and now hobbled his way up West Lane wheeling a battered pram containing a wind-up gramophone, which he propelled around the village playing scratchy martial music and old-time music hall songs.

How he came to settle in the combe, I don't know, but he was not a born local and therefore considered a foreigner by the bona fide villagers. They avoided him whenever they could ("Watch out, ol' Pegleg's comin', mad ol' bugger," and they would scuttle for refuge). Any caught out would smile nervously and, avoiding eye contact, toss him a few pence before moving quickly on. Somehow though, he managed to meet and seduce into marrying him, Vera Smith, a village maiden; perhaps because Vera was grossly obese and with swollen purply legs, lank mousy hair and bland, unmemorable features. ("Ee's er only 'ope, fer zure.")

Vera wore a lank, tent-sized linen dress which hung limply over her lumpish body like a shroud, worn-down sandals below swollen ankles. Her expression was always sad. Seeing her waddling slowly up West Lane with her grocery basket, we children would snigger cruelly behind her back. ("Er's a bit simple, you know, a bit slow on the uptake.") Whether that was true, I don't know; I never heard her speak. But people can be cruel, including myself. The image of her and Bob copulating, if they ever did, defied the imagination.

Misconceptions formed through ignorance and bigotry take pleasure in their own spitefulness. Maybe Bob and Vera, both dealt a duff hand by the gods, mocked by their fellow beings, discovered in each other some higher alchemy of the soul, a kindred spirit of tenderness and constancy; in essence, sharing that most elusive and cherished of all rapturous states: true love. Or maybe not. Who knows?

* * * * *

Next door to Pegleg lived Bill Baker. Bill's garden ran parallel with the top of the bank and here he cultivated vegetables, fruit trees, too: apples, pears, and plums. On the way home from school on sunny autumn afternoons we would see him. Short in stature, his face weathered, with ancient eyes that twinkled rheumily, his nose bubbled as he spoke, spraying a misty film which trickled down into a matted grey moustache that harboured, we suspected, things unsavoury. Beneath it, his false teeth clattered as he spoke. He seemed lost in shapeless clothes: dark yarn trousers, a grubby collarless shirt, waistcoat and watch chain, heedless of the weather. He would smile broadly at us and come to the edge of the bank.

"Would ee like zome apples, m'dears? Would ee like zum, zur nuff?" And he would throw some down to us.

"Has ee ever asked ee in?" our parents queried anxiously when we told them, then added, enigmatically, "Don't ee ever go een ee's 'ouse, mind!" We'd be bemused when they failed to elaborate, our fertile fancies extending to whimsical proportions.

"Ee's got children caged up een there, fat'nin' 'em up, like the witch in Hansel and Gretel. Gonna eat 'em!"

Of Bill's early life, I know nothing. He must once have been young – as must Archie and Pegleg, impossible as that seemed to us – back in the days before motor cars when they all rode horses, and wolves roamed the land, and we would dream of living then, too: no school, whoopee! Bill seemed antediluvian.

Eventually he died. Dennis's mother, old Mrs Madge from Rock Cottage, and Archie's wife, had the dubious duty of cleaning and dressing the body, laying it out.

"Did ee hiver see such a state?" they exclaimed of his cottage. (No caged and fattened children, then. We were disappointed.) "Ee's feet," they said. "Most've the skin came away wi' ee's socks! Goodness knows ow long ee'd been wearin' 'em. As fer the rest of un... Well, less said the better. Did ee hiver zee ought like it?"

THE VILLAGE

Dolton village lay at the head of the valley, a cluster of cob and thatched cottages angled around the village square and lining the high street. A pub, the Royal Oak, faced onto the square adjoining the school and its cobbled playground. From there, an antiquated and darkly intimidating wooden door barricaded access to the churchyard, wherein the graves of Dolton inhabitants over the centuries surrounded the stone-built church itself.

Fields and copses, farms and their tied cottages – seemingly sprouting like fungi from the land – surrounded the village. Skyline ridges, hidden troughs and rifts and stony lanes sunken between shady hedgerow and traversed over the centuries by cattle, sheep, geese, and men, wound their labyrinthine way through wood and meadow, circumventing swamps and bogs to terminate at lonely farmhouses. Brooks and rills twined their tortuous routes to the valley floor, occasionally intersecting at some point, all on their way to the river.

The village too, cosseted secret places: unseen gardens behind high stone walls over which the top boughs of fruit trees tantalizingly dangled their seductive wares; alleyways leading to rustic barns and disused stables at the end of which elegant houses stood haughtily forbidding behind cobbled courtyards, and from which we children would turn and silently slink away. Doors of solid, ancient, and creosoted wood cracked and warped by the elements of centuries lay deep-set in bulging cob walls through whose dark apertures we would peer warily, only to see dust and shadows and smell the crabbed scents of a past age.

The whole of the parish held a population of only a few hundred, each of whom knew the other, if not intimately, then by sight, or by their dogs. Outlying farmers, jodhpured and gaitered, and wearing grease-stained trilbies or ratting caps, would visit the village stores; the pubs, too. Their labourers also; blue overalls over collarless shirts, hobnailed boots, or wellingtons, faces red and weather-etched. They would gossip easily and amiably with the village artisans and traders, each familiar with the others' lives as a largely self-supporting unit. Chapel-going Methodists, while disapproving of drink, would benevolently accept the Anglicans and seculars who haunted the spiritually suspect establishments, and would co-exist tolerantly.

As in all communities, there were petty feuds but, in ours at least, no violence or discernible crime. One police constable served both us and the neighbouring village of Beaford where he was based, but I never heard mention of his presence or name, nor ever remember seeing him.

At this particular time in place and history, in deepest Devon, people were still mostly or distantly related, insular, and suspicious of foreigners – the latter being anyone north-east of Exeter or south of Okehampton. The old folk still wondered what the world was coming to, while, in this immediate post-war era, the young eagerly anticipated a new golden age.

✴ ✴ ✴ ✴ ✴

There was a pecking order dictated by age amongst we children. At the top, for we boys, were those who had recently left school but were not yet fully adult (today they would be referred to as teenagers). These, we younger ones would look up to respectfully and with a tinge of awe. We would follow them on illicit forays to the trenches and firing ranges used for training by the Home Guard on outlying hillsides, where we would pretend to be soldiers; or would accompany them on bicycle trips to Winkleigh aerodrome, some five miles away. There, we spied on the airbase, gazing in wonder at the huge transports thundering along runways before growling harshly into the night sky: a sight never before seen by any villager.

＊ ＊ ＊ ＊ ＊

In farming communities, sex was ever-present; the bull would be taken to the cow, the stallion to the mare; sheep would be raddled by the ram, and the rooster would strut possessively amongst the hens: so too the humans, albeit more judiciously and, in most cases, selectively.

Our village was no different. An undercurrent of sexual cupidity rippled through its unmarried youth (and some married, too). Degrees of passion mingled with a more prosaic disillusionment behind the closed doors of the connubial, presupposed publicly only by rumour and innuendo. The former were more open; flirtations and courtships, rivalries, and jealousies. Passion and romance and graduations of lustful activity ranged from a furtive kiss in a quiet lane to the more energetically awkward contortions in haylofts and secluded arbours.

On the school bus home, a couple of the more forward boys would grin knowingly, smugly brag of having 'gone all the way' with some girl or other. Wide-eyed, half-believing, we more naive would say, "But won't er 'ave a baby?"

"Git out wi' ee," they would laugh, condescendingly, "I weared a johnnie 'f course."

A johnnie? I'd heard of them. Once, I'd actually spotted a discarded one in a field from where I'd seen a couple, furtive in the dark the night before, leaving the gateway. I recognised the girl, but couldn't believe ... And yet ... Did they?

Michael Wilson, who was a few years older than me and beyond the leaving age of fifteen but still at school until the end of term, was tall and good-looking. He had always been kind to me when walking home from primary school, siding with me against Doris before veering off to his home at Lock's Hill. He possessed a luscious head of black, slickly Brylcreemed hair, from which, on breezy days, wayward locks fell over his face to below his chin. This highly impressed me. It was just like the city slickers, gangsters in *Brighton Rock*, which we had seen in the weekly mobile picture show in Dolton village hall.

Dad always cut my hair, no-nonsense short back and sides, army style.

"Can't I grow it long, Dad? Like the big boys," I'd complain.

"No, you can't, you'll have it cut respectable, neat and proper." Dad was conservative in every way.

"But Michael Wilson has his long."

"You're not Michael Wilson."

And that was that.

But Michael Wilson's good looks and sleek, city-slicker Brylcreemed locks seemed to have paid off, because, as a spidery-thin, gauche first-year pupil at secondary school, I felt a twinge of envy when I spotted him in the long grass at the edge of the playing field, shiny locks falling like ebony snakes across the face of a girl lying supine beneath him. They were kissing passionately, both fully clothed as far as I could ascertain through the tiger-striped grass.

Several years later, there was a spate of shocked village gossip when Michael courted a girl somewhat younger than he. However, they eventually married and remained the rest of their lives and into old age in the village, becoming a respectable and venerated couple.

* * * * *

On bitter winter days of black ice and incumbent grey skies, with dead leaves wind-blown in sludge-frozen gutters, we children would, during our dinner hour, descend upon the village forge to watch the horse-shoeing, and be blasted by heat from the roaring furnace as it softened the iron being hammered into shape ready for fitting by Lloyd Wilson the blacksmith, Michael's father. Doubled over the massive hoof of a Shire horse clasped between his leather-protected thighs, he would use long pliers to dip the red-hot shoe, angrily hissing, into a bucket of cold water before expertly nailing it onto the crusty, nerveless fibre of the hoof.

We would watch fascinated, then, job complete, would make our hunch-shouldered way back to school.

＊ ＊ ＊ ＊ ＊

In a small, whitewashed cottage, Bill Baily lived with his mother and their parrot. Bill had been a sailor, a Royal Navy stoker, had seen the world and returned home surprisingly unworldly. He was sturdy and benign and spent his days, during opening hours, in the Royal Oak. I remember him as being softly spoken, shy and kind. Of his mother I have only a hazy memory; a tiny, grey-haired old lady, seldom seen outside their cottage. The parrot – presumably purchased by Bill in some distant port – perched in its cage on the window-seat, an exotic addition to the village upon which it gazed with a beady and inscrutable eye. I would glance at it in passing, a large, impossibly emblazoned, gaudy creature, and for a fanciful moment have visions of tropical islands, steaming jungles, and lost cities deep in equatorial Africa, such as I had read about in my comics and books.

Then one day, tragedy. Fire. Its cause I've long forgotten. Ugly orange and yellow flames, crackling and spitting malignantly, writhing and contorting like fiery fiends behind a pall of billowing, odoriferous smoke.

Bill and his mother were saved but their parrot was not. Its demise affected me deeply: a brilliant and sentient jewel from a land of legend, destroyed so randomly. I tried not to think about it too much.

✻ ✻ ✻ ✻ ✻

Reuben Knott was short and stocky, sturdy as an English oak and with a kindly face creased and tanned as mellowed leather. He was softly spoken, with a deep Devon intonation such as is seldom heard nowadays. Rube was the drasher (thrasher) man.

"Us be drashin' today," would go the cry of contingent farms. And Reuben would set off with his son Tom and their fierce-eyed Jack Russell terrier, in their old steam traction engine, chuffing and puffing and surrounded by a miasma of oil fumes, its tyre-less iron wheels churning up the tarmac of country roads and towing the dusty corn thrasher, sending startled cattle, horses and sheep to far corners of their fields.

✻ ✻ ✻ ✻ ✻

Thrashing was a communal event, with neighbouring farmers and their labourers turning up to help. The traction engine powered the thrasher via a sturdy canvas belt, throbbing and pulsating.

"Don't ee go near thiky belt, mind," Rube would warn any spectating children. "Ee'll make mince-meat of ee, sure nuff." As if to emphasise Rube's warning the belt would whump and jerk as though to escape its spinning drum, before settling down again. Atop the rick, men would pass sheaves of corn into the humming, clunking machine; others below bagging the emerging grain. A veil of swirling dust and chaff soon coated their attire, clogging their noses and irritating their eyes, and filling the air with the dry scent of milled corn and swirling, discarded husks.

At midday, women folk arrived, staggering under the weight of hampers containing pies and flans, sandwiches, and cakes, sweet, non-alcoholic (being chapel people) cider, and a blessed silence descended. The dust cleared and cheerful chatter and banter filled the air.

Later, as the rick diminished to a few feet above the ground, the rats began to bolt, dozens of them fleeing in panic from disturbed nests and lairs, and the slaughter began. Reuben's Jack Russell, sturdy as his master, now came into his own. Fast as a bobcat, a blur of black and white, a lethal and ruthless killer, he dashed and spun, first one rat then another was seized by the scruff of the neck and emitted a short, shrill, and terrified squeal before its broken-necked body was flung spinning in an arc, even as its slayer pounced onto another victim. Meanwhile, the normally mild and placid workers became animated assassins, stamping and yelling, crushing, and wounding rats at random, ululating and brandishing them high, squirming and squealing, impaled upon pitchforks.

"Argh! The bugger's run up me trouser leg!" A worker, having neglected to fasten baler cord around the bottoms of his trouser legs, frantically grabbed the squirming bulge blindly scrabbling its way towards his groin, crushing, strangling it, desperate to prevent any further ascent.

"You nearly lost 'em there, Frank," someone chortled to much raucous laughter.

"Giddout, do ee's missus a favour," another jibed.

"Bit below the belt, thiky," exclaimed another, to a further gust of hilarity. And Frank gingerly worked the strangled rodent to the bottom of his trouser leg to cast it, in disgust, as far away as possible. It would most likely be dusk before the thrashing was finished, and Rube and Tom, the terrier beside them in the traction engine cab, would puff and chuff their way slowly home in the soft autumn night.

✻ ✻ ✻ ✻ ✻

Jackson was an itinerant farm labourer referred to only as 'Jackson', although I assume he had a Christian name. He lived somewhere on the outskirts of Dolton, a barn or outhouse maybe, accommodated in a farmhouse spare room in return for his labour. He was ubiquitous at harvest time, taddy-picking-up, thrashing, and other annual rituals on the surrounding farms. Weather-beaten and unshaven, lean, and sinewy and wearing a soiled gabardine mackintosh, articulating in a broad Devon accent, he would often arrive, dusty and thirsty at the Royal Oak on horseback, seeming the last echo of an earlier age. His origins were obscure. As with other local eccentrics, he will be long gone now, largely forgotten.

✻ ✻ ✻ ✻ ✻

To me, of all the girls in the village, the Horrell sisters stand out. They were pretty, dark-haired, and flashing-eyed, feisty, and alluring. They lived with their parents and brother Kenny in a small whitewashed cottage at the top of West Lane. There were four of them as I remember: Annie, Jean, Ruth, and Pamela. The latter two were nearest me in age with Kenny squeezed somewhere in between. They were an abundant target for gossip, warranted or otherwise, with their handsome looks and mercurial presence, their irrepressibility. They coursed through the village setting many a male heart aflutter. They flirted seductively, fragrantly. Their effervescent and passionate natures quickened male hearts, inflated chests and egos and were a force for gaiety and light. I remember them as I remember sunlit fields and snow-dazzled winter lanes: sharp and bright and a sweet breath of life, ever young and vital and of their time. To their charms I was not immune. But as I left the parish at sixteen, any deeper involvement with them, sadly, never developed, and I know little of their future lives, fortunes, joys, or despairs.

In retrospect I think they may have had an elder brother, Neil. He would have been older than me, already an adult, and I only recall the name, Neil Horrell, (not such a common name as not to be related in such a small village) because of a tragic event. Dad and I were going to Dolton one Saturday evening. It was before the inception of the travelling picture show and we were going to spend the evening with Harry Jury, the village carpenter and Dad's friend. It was late autumn, windless and already dark, a fine mist silently creeping up from the valley floor.

"Be ee off to Dolton, then?" asked Mr Friend, emerging from his shed.

Dad concurred.

"I wouldn't go Langham way if I wuz you."

"No?" Dad waited for the expected quip.

"Been an accident."

"Ha …" Dad grinned, pausing.

"Pretty nasty, I yur."

We waited.

"Couple'a bays killed."

Killed? He couldn't be joking, surely, and yet … not up Langham road, horrors like that didn't happen there.

"So I'm told. Tis true, 'pparently. Motorbike and a lorry. Purtty messy by all accounts."

"Is that right, Bob?" said Dad, sombre now.

"Oh, aye, tis right sure nuff."

So we went via the farm lane, stony and pitted, winding dark between high hedgerows and woodland which cast threatening shadows across our weak bike-light beams, avoiding Langham Road and eventually emerging into West Lane. The news had already reached the village: two boys on a motorbike had been on their way to Hatherleigh. Langham Road was a narrow B-road, one-lane and winding its way down to the river bridge in the valley. The boys were in a head-on collision with a forestry lorry. They were going fast. The lorry was huge and solid, loaded along its length with large tree trunks. They had no chance. Their mangled bodies were wrapped beneath the lorry, torn and mashed along its undercarriage.

Frank Squires, a farmer, Methodist preacher, and Evelyn's father, had been working in a nearby field and was first on the scene. He hurried to his farmhouse a quarter of a mile away, to phone the ambulance and police, although the boys were obviously dead. The feelings of Neil Horrell left alone on a country road with the shattered motorbike, the dismembered human remains still warm and dripping beneath his lorry, one can only surmise. He knew the boys, would have known who they were. One, Ray Hutchings, was a Dolton resident he would have known well. The other, David Coppledick, came from Hatherleigh. I knew them both.

MAYFLOWER MORNING & HAWHIP AFTERNOON

WINTER

Christmas had gone and the world was dead. Beyond hearth and home, all was uniform grey; the trees skeletal, stripped of life. Brambles, brown and brittle, crunched like dry bones underfoot. The bloated river rumbled sullenly through the valley and birdsong was scant and muted. Once-green fields presented naked brown soil to an indifferent sky as an endless bleak wind scoured the earth. And the colour of death was not black, but brown.

We scurried, heads down and collars up, from school bus to home, and from home to school bus again the following morning. On Saturday, well-wrapped, we ventured outdoors.

"What shall us do?" asked Trevor.

"Dunno," I said.

Don't go near the river, we had been warned. So we did; walking its ragged banks as closely as we dared, kicking at bank overhangs until they rumbled in a miniature landslide into the turgid current and leaping back onto solid terrain as they did so. Only Micky, as usual enjoying himself, was seemingly immune to the biting cold as we ran through a dismal woodland of dead leaves, slithered and skidded into a field where rain-swept turnips protruded from the mud like gruesome human skulls. We wrenched one from the earth. It tasted of mud and pepper.

"My fingers've gone numb," winced Trevor.

"My hands is freezin'," I said.

So we went home.

* * * * *

On the way to Sunday school the wind strummed a dirge on the telephone wires. Coming home there was no wind, complete silence.

Something was about to happen.

Then it struck me. "The sky…" I exclaimed to Valerie. "It's going to snow!"

And we laughed and skipped joyously the rest of the way home.

* * * * *

That night I lay by candlelight, watching spellbound as snowflakes spiralled like ghost-moths outside my bedroom window. Next morning, under a glacial sun, a wondrous white blanket covered the land; diamond prisms shimmered and sparkled like ice-stars fallen to earth. Virgin snow lay seamless over the lane. There would be no thaw today. We waited, but the school bus never came. A stolen day of enchantment lay ahead.

Later, Valerie and I flamingo-stepped through the snow, frozen dragon-breath flaring from our mouths and nostrils. Our fingers and toes tingled. Micky, mystified and excited, bounced and sprang ahead of us, snow gathering in furry clumps around his paws. Ponds were frozen; when we tentatively stepped onto the ice it crackled ominously and we backed off smartly.

"Look!" exclaimed Valerie.

I looked. A solitary tear, a snowdrop, white as the snow and emerald-tinted, nodded contentedly in a frozen landscape, a promise of the coming spring.

SPRING

But soon the snow was gone as mysteriously as it had arrived. The wind swung around to the southwest and grey clouds with sullen faces loomed over the distant moor to eddy towards us. And with it came the rain, mist and drizzle. What passed for daylight weakly surrendered to tarnished night, and we were scornful to be assured that the days were getting longer.

But they were.

And I awoke one morning to blue sky and a fluttering outside my bedroom window. A dark shape flashed past, accompanied by excited chittering, sharp as crystal, and I realized, with a surge of excitement, that the house martins had returned from their epic journey across two continents, sporting an aurora of fragile pink and embracing sunlight in all its dazzling glory.

Outdoors, the snowdrops were losing their lustre, to be replaced by primroses, gay in the hedgerows, buttercream faces laughing in the sunlight. Trees were bursting into leaf and the whole countryside exploding into joyous life. I cycled to collect our milk, still warm from the morning's milking at Home Farm. Then, checking the lid was secure on our milk-can, carefully suspended it from my handlebars before setting off homeward.

The long lane to the main road was bordered by expansive fields, some with tiny green blades of wheat spearing boldly from the earth, others grazed by sheep with heavy wool soon to be shorn, or ruby-red cattle, harem to a muscular bull. The air was pleasantly warm and a light breeze nudged scents from the hedgerows, a perfumed whisper of wildflowers, and I free-wheeled down to a slight dip where, towering before me like a clipper ship under full sail, was the old hawthorn tree, gnarled and contorted at its base, an explosion of white mayflower billowing above it, edged by an aurora of fragile pink and embracing the sunlight in all its dazzling glory. And in that one perspicacious moment, all the light and excitement of the summer ahead was compressed within me into an instant of joy

SUMMER

We listened to the school bus rumble away into the distance, leaving just birdsong and the sun warm on our faces. Six joyous weeks of freedom stretched ahead: the school summer holidays. Below us the valley shimmered; a veiled Enid Blyton landscape of lost caves and hidden secrets awaiting our discovery. Green fields dotted with sheep and cattle, cornfields of muted gold, lay spread like a quilt of many colours along its slopes, while way below flashes of shattered crystal from the river could be glimpsed between its tree-lined banks.

I would be given the occasional holiday chore: weeding, or cleaning out the chicken shed pungent with ammonia, picking peas or beans for dinner; all of which I did with ill grace, muttering, eager to be off exploring with Trevor and Micky.

Once free we would disappear, setting off to discover seldom visited woodland inhabited by secretive creatures, shy of humans and living their hidden lives in chequered shade beneath a rustling canopy of birdsong.

Here we built a flimsy camp of hazel wands, twigs and ferns, before dispersing to discover mysterious mounds, half-buried beneath moss and creeping ivy. On closer inspection they appeared to be the remains of a dry-stone wall which, with increasing excitement and curiosity, we traced through the trees. Whose long-dead hands had laid these stones? Leaves shimmied, elegant ferns whispered, and the ancient wildwood quietly retained the ghosts of a lost settlement within its bosom.

Torpid August rain fell, dampening our spirits as well as the corn, and releasing pungent scents to hang heavy in the air. Steam arose from field and hedgerow. The rain cascaded from leaves to fall with dull staccato beat to the woodland floor. Ferns bowed and danced beneath its weight, brambles hissed; their ripening fruit, freshly cleansed, glistened.

Trevor and I huddled impatiently in our camp, an undersea grotto of nebulous liquid green, until finally the watery drum-roll abated, the greenery lightened, and we glanced up hopefully. Our hearts lifted at a patch of blue glimpsed through the leafy canopy. A buzzard soared, mewled. Sunlight shimmered through the leaves to fall around us.

In the bed of the valley, between banks of hazel and elder, ran the river. Interspersed between the banks were occasional gullies, mud-churned by cattle going to drink, when they would linger awhile in the shaded coolness, swishing their brush-ended tails to disperse blood-hungry horseflies from their rumps. A long, narrow flood plain of coarse tufted grass, grazed by the cattle, divided the river from a rush-covered marshland which lined the rim of the woods.

Sunlight created bejewelled raindrops clinging to overhead leaves to fall around us and, upon leaving our camp, to this marsh we descended. Once in the open, the sun beat savagely on our backs. Steam rose, eddied, and faded in the fierce heat. A mordant bog-smell, odoriferous and infested by midges and mosquitoes, hovered between tall clumps of reeds, and beneath our feet the earth gurgled unstably, but, like good redskin scouts, we knew its secret trails and adhered confidently and diligently to them. Beyond the plain, the siren-song of the river called invitingly.

"Swimmin' s'afternoon?" I suggested.

"Yeah! Let's dive for pearls off the fallen log," said Trevor.

"Pearls?"

"Yeah ... well, you never know," Trevor said.

AUTUMN

With the summer holidays now becoming a distant memory, the corn mostly gathered in and flocks of woodpigeons waddling, seeking fallen grain amongst the dusty golden stubble, ricks being thatched, and roadside hedges being trimmed, harvest festivals just around the corner and the days becoming noticeably shorter, autumn came creeping in.

Soon the stubble will vanish, fields will be turned inside-out by the plough; dusty gold being transformed to ridged rows of dark brown like a turbid, petrified sea. Some ploughs of more than one shear are drawn by a staccato-harsh tractor, others of a single shear by a steaming Shire horse snorting clouds of misted breath and followed by a sturdy ploughman with arms of knotted muscle guiding the plough: fading echoes of a past era. Behind them, motes against a frigid sky, come flocks of strident rooks and shrieking seagulls to jostle in a frenzied body over nakedly exposed worms, grubs, and leatherjackets.

In grazing pastures, awakening vaguely-dreamed, half-believed myths of elf and fairy rings, field mushrooms magically appear overnight, creamy pristine white heads shy in the grass; plump, off-white puffballs exploding dusty spores beneath the cloven hooves of cattle.

In the woodlands the canopy of leaves will be turning a melting pastel of soft colours, some floating dreamingly to the forest floor where a variety of mysterious fungi now sprout, all shapes, sizes, and hues, growing on tree trunks or fallen rotting wood, others peeking warily from leaf mould; some edible, some not. Veiled shadow lurks enigmatically between tree trunks, elusive shapes seen from the corner of the eye; misty pillars of light lie spectrally in the far reaches, and an omnipresent silence hints at ambush.

In field and roadside hedgerows hazel nuts are browning in their cups, purple sloes ripening upon blackthorn, blood-red haw hips like plump rubies on the hawthorn. We children, on our trek home from school, whack the hazel to topple ripe nuts to the ground, then risk our teeth by using them as nut crackers. Sometimes a kernel contains a grub and we choke disgustedly and disgorge it in a stream of saliva, to the general hilarity of the others. The fruit of the blackthorn, too, we bite bravely into, screwing our faces grotesquely at the bitter taste, but spit out the stone and persevere anyway, see who can last the longest. We are attracted to the scarlet haw hips like tears of blood on the hawthorn, but know they are inedible.

Dusk is already sneaking in, so we jog and trot off home to tea and *Children's Hour* on the wireless.

THE MISS BUDDS

Leaving the combe, the brook weaved its way through a boggy wasteland under the shadow of Halsdon Wood, where old animal bones and ribcages protruded half-sunken from the ooze like landlocked shipwrecks (combe dwellers seldom disposed of their deceased livestock according to law). Crystal-clear now and gurgling happily, the brook hugged the base of the dark woodland as it penetrated ever deeper into ancient leas and tumbled, untended forgotten hedgerows. Finally it reached the old mill, isolated and crumbling, its rotting millwheel long stilled.

Nearby and slightly elevated, stood the mill-house, a large farmhouse, and with a front door bordered by rambling red roses. A lawn and flower garden fronted it, separated from the stony farmyard by iron railings. The front door was no longer used; instead, three worn stone steps led up to a side door direct from the farmyard, leading into a spacious pantry in which were large oak beams, darkened by age and smoke from an open fire and studded with three iron hooks for suspending game, poultry and pig carcasses. A well-scrubbed wooden farmhouse table was littered with various household implements. On the flagstone floor stood farm implements, including milking stools, buckets and an old clothes mangle.

A door led into a living room containing another wooden table, some seating forms and a 19th century dresser containing china knick-knacks of the same vintage. A well-used sofa and armchairs of a floral design rested beneath the window.

The rest of the house was seldom used and only ever visited by the resident sisters. Doors led deeper into other rooms of increasing silence and the scent of wood polish and old books secreting pressed flowers from a passed era. Dust motes swam lazily in shafts of sunlight penetrating the windows. Undisturbed air hung still as time suspended, within which the aura of past centuries and hovering ghosts lay heavy.

Once, the mill had been a hive of rustic industry; cartloads of grain hauled by huge, steaming Shire horses had wound their way through the woods and down the steep lanes to converge there. A hum of activity, swirling husks of corn-dust and the splish-splash of the millwheel, the clanking, grinding machinery and the ubiquitous voices and laughter of farm and mill workers. Ducks swam in the brook, geese preened themselves on its banks and eels writhed glistening black in the water. A wooden bridge spanned the brook, sturdy enough to be traversed by carts and wains on the way to a further mill on the banks of the river.

On the far side of the bridge lay a long-abandoned garden, its provenance revealed now only by a gangling tangle of raspberry canes protruding from long grass and nascent saplings on either side of the path at the top of which, before turning sharp left to join the main track to the mill, stood a cob ruin. Its chimney pointed poignantly, like a gnarled finger, into tumbling woodland in which invasive rhododendron shrubs divulged the existence of Victorian horticulture long reclaimed by the Green Man. Once a small 'dye house', then a labourer's cottage, the ruin was slowly losing its battle with the elements.

This was all before my time, of course, relayed to me by the two Miss Budds, spinster daughters of the last miller. They now lived alone in the farmhouse, tending a few cows and sheep, chickens and ducks. They worked their few fields, mainly just hay for their cattle or grazing for their sheep, the fields being too low and prone to flooding for cultivation. The mill itself, long silent, was roofless and crumbling, alder and rowan sprouting from its remaining cob walls. A forest of nettles strangled the corroding machinery, a haven for tits, wrens and blackbirds, their songs replacing the echoes of a long-passed industry. The wooden bridge, gradually being washed away by floodwaters, had gaping holes and exposed struts across which Trevor and I balanced like tightrope walkers, as Micky swam below.

The two sisters resembled each other not at all. There was 'Outdoor' sister and 'Indoor' sister. The former was lean and stringy, her leathery face resembling a knobbly potato, the latter, sweet-faced, must once, when young, have been exceptionally pretty. She had been crippled by polio as a child, and maybe that's why she never married, her sister remaining loyally as carer. Not that 'Indoor' was idle. She tended the house, made butter and cream, cooked the meals, and made cakes and bread. 'Outdoor' tended the livestock, toiled in the fields and sheds. Both spoke with a surprisingly articulate and intelligible accent.

The farmyard resembled a bucolic idyll; chickens and ducks scratched, pecked, and foraged, and the occasional ewe and her new-born lamb mingled with the milk cows and their calves which were herded in from the lea twice a day for milking. The calves, fathered by the bull of a neighbouring farm, when weaned were sold on at market. Each cow had its individual name and was treated fondly, spoken to gently and never saw a market. A chicken or duck would occasionally be killed for the pot, the sisters being born and bred as practical, not overly-sentimental, countrywomen. I knew them well, and now wish I had further picked their brains and memories for the wealth of living history they possessed.

During summer, every Friday evening, I walked with Dad and Micky along the high lanes and down through the woods to the old mill, where Dad would present a basket of asparagus from his garden for 'Outdoors' Miss Budd to take to Okehampton street market the next day. Often, the sun would be setting, the river glinting silver through the trees and the brook murmuring silkily as shades of night fell and the chickens were ambling off to roost. Mist rose from the river and the trees whispered conspiratorially as a warm glow of peace and tranquillity encompassed me.

Early Saturday mornings, Pat Knight's taxi, from Dolton, would rock and rumble in low gear along the lanes to park at the top of the woods, when he would descend to help Miss Budd carry her produce of eggs, butter, fruit, and honey – and asparagus – up before conveying her to Higher Lodge, where she would catch the bus in to Okehampton.

The old mill had a vegetable and fruit garden, largely overgrown, in which Dad would labour, digging and tilling, cutting back fruit canes, pruning and hoeing – for a fee, I presume. At the end of the garden was a high stone alcove which, looking back, was probably a disused lime kiln. Along the bank beside it were three bee hives which 'Outdoors' tended, using the appropriate bee-keeper's outfit. During weekends and school summer holidays, when the air lay heavy and thunder threatened, I would be paid a half-crown to sit at the edge of the bank armed with a heavy iron bell to ring should the bees swarm. Under such conditions the bees were liable to swarm and fly off into the wild blue yonder. Vibrations from the ringing bell, apparently, calmed them down. It was the most boring of jobs, and sometimes Trevor would appear for a while to sit with me, but soon made some excuse and wandered off.

One day, with thunder rumbling and ominous dark clouds approaching from the south, I noticed an increase in the timbre of the bees: wilder, premonitory. They flocked thicker, denser, swirled, and dipped in an increasingly spinning configuration, a darkening and amorphous cloud. They were swarming, I knew they were. I should ring the bell. But what if I were wrong? I would look a fool. I hesitated. Suddenly, a lean and scrawny figure came hurtling down the path from the farmhouse, one hand holding down a straw bonnet above a knobbly red face.

"The bell, Allan, ring the bell, they're swarming!"

Even as she started to speak, I jumped to my feet and clanged the bell like a town crier with a firework up his trouser-leg, telling myself perhaps she would think I had been ringing it all the time and she hadn't heard. Idiot! Miss Budd stood in the garden below, anxiously watching and crooning. Slowly the frantic buzzing lessened, the cloud broke up, separated.

"Didn't you see them, Allan?"

"Yes, but... I ... I thought..."

I felt my face burning with embarrassment. What would she think? I'd been asleep? I deliberately let them swarm? Would I still get my half-crown? I never found out what she thought. She was too kind and polite to do more than say gently, "When they swarm, they'll take off for miles, settle anywhere, and I could lose them." I got my half-crown, plus a honey and cream tea.

Early one humid summer's evening rain fell in blankets. It battered our cottage windows, pounded the garden flat and drum-rolled atop Micky's kennel. When it eased we could hear the angry growl of the river and gazed out to see it sweeping over the meadows below, muddied, the colour of thick tea. Meanwhile, down in the combe, I heard later, it had burst its banks and crashed its way up the brook like a tidal bore, through the low woodland into the Miss Budds' garden, uprooting vegetables, and fruit canes, snatching up the bee hives and transporting them downstream, tumbling and twisting, crashing against fallen trees and stony banks, breaking them apart. What happened to the bees? I can't remember. Did they drown? Did they take off in a swarm? Flee to safety? Return? I felt sorry for the two sisters. They were as fond of their bees, in a way, as they were of their other livestock.

Some years later, owing to advancing years and ill health, they sold the old mill and moved to a house in nearby Hatherleigh, which must have been heartbreaking for them, the old mill having been in the family since the 18th century. Dad said I should visit them, they'd be delighted to see me, but sadly I never got around to it, so never saw them again, much to my now regret.

POST SCHOOL

"Have you got a job, Allan?" asked Evelyn.

I had always liked Evelyn. Her best friend, Elaine, a shy and slight, frizzly-haired girl who wore glasses, was in love with me. But I rather fancied Evelyn, or Elaine's sister, Maureen, both the latter being, how can I say, rather more developed, and exuding that air of nascent and mysterious voluptuousness so magnetic to a schoolboy. Little Elaine had some catching up to do. I knew Elaine was in love with me because the other two teased her about it when I was within earshot. Elaine would shuffle and blush, eyes huge and wide behind her glasses. I in turn, was teased about it by my friends.

"Daft ol' maid," I'd mutter, reddening.

Evelyn asked me this after the 'bell' on our very last day at Torrington Secondary Modern School as we rose and headed in the general rush for the classroom door. It was a fine day outside, spring in the air and three weeks' Easter holiday to look forward to – for some, but not for me.

"Yeah," I replied, "on a farm." I was slightly embarrassed at this, being the equivalent of 'At t' mill,' in Lancashire: common as muck! I felt I'd let myself down in her eyes. But we were through the door by this time, fanning out amidst the others, all heading for our respective school buses, and I never had time to reciprocate the question.

If ever asked, "Do ee like skewel, bay?" It was obligatory to scoff derisively and reply, "No!" Anything else and you were a bit odd, a swot or worse. Yet on this last day, although I would never admit it, I wasn't nearly so sure; it hadn't been so bad, really. My immediate thought being no more summer dinner breaks, it being too hot for football, lazing on the grassy bank in the warmth of the sun with Dennis and my other friends, joking and jousting; even the teasing, in retrospect, seemed strangely pleasurable. Somehow, the three girls would contrive to be nearby, glancing our way, occasionally giggling and whispering furtively, good-hearted.

"Er fancies you, Al, better go'n sit next to er."

"Don't talk daft!"

"Git on, you loves er, really."

"What! Don't be so daft! Bloomin' ol' maid."

Sports lessons, on the way back from football (at which I was useless), I would see the girls playing netball, devoid of their skirts, their white blouses tucked into the voluminous navy-blue knickers schoolgirls wore back then, and my eyes would linger furtively. Evelyn in particular, well-developed for her age, possessed a gracefully symmetrical bottom, and as she stretched to place the ball through the net her breasts thrust tightly beneath her blouse, eliciting a pleasant sensation in my chest which I couldn't really explain. No; overall, omitting the week of sweating terror when the school dentist was in attendance and we didn't get appointments but could be summoned to our fate at any moment, school hadn't been so bad. And somehow I would miss the three girls. I never did see any of them again. They will now, like me, be in the autumn of their lives and I would dearly love to meet them once more. Although maybe not: three fresh, golden young girls on the cusp of womanhood, now post-menopause, elderly ladies… Best, perhaps, to cherish the memory.

✳ ✳ ✳ ✳ ✳

And so began my first job at Higher Langham Farm, under the tenancy of the Squires family. I had once creosoted the roof of their henhouse for five bob, then broken out in an allergic rash for my pains. Each year Dad helped them with the corn harvest in return for grain for our chickens, picking up taddies for receipt of a couple of rows in their field, barter being very much still alive in those post-war years.

The family consisted of the farmer, his wife and two daughters and a much younger son, plus son-in-law Bill, who had planned on joining the RAF; his plans seriously thwarted by his impregnation of the eldest daughter, another Evelyn, a raven-haired, dark-eyed beauty with pale skin, smooth as porcelain and a body which oozed femininity and fecundity, the latter being verified by a shotgun wedding and a stream of further births.

Farmer Squires was in his fifties at the time, freckle-featured, with greying red hair and a moustache. He was soft and slow-spoken, a kindly man whom I never saw lose his temper, despite being often provoked by Bill, who after the wedding came to live and work on the farm. Underpaid and overworked, he'd complain, half-jokingly.

"Never git married, bay," he would passionately advise me. His two false front teeth flicked out, then clicked back again as he spoke. He was loud and vivacious, skittish and volatile, and often at odds with his father-in-law who, to Bill's frustration, remained ever calm and placid and always seemed to come out on top.

Eileen was a different matter. Younger sister to Evelyn, but with the misfortune not to share her sister's good looks, she allegedly suffered from some heart problem which precluded her from any heavy tasks. Twenty-two at the time, she was skinny, sallow, and sharp-featured with a prominent nose and thin-lipped mouth, which would contort with sarcasm and belligerence every time she spoke to Bill who, for some inexplicable reason, she disliked, and they would go at it hammer and tongs. Her favourite spot was a low stool beside the large open fireplace where, at eleven o'clock, she would hunker down with a cup of tea, jerking and fidgeting around whilst engaging Bill in verbal battle as I, sitting quietly opposite with the three farm dogs nudging me hopefully as I ate my lunchtime cheese sandwich, tried furtively to peer up her skirt for what turned out to be a momentary glimpse of disappointingly voluminous bloomers.

Francis, the first-born son, was reported missing, believed dead, in WWII. I never knew him, but his name once briefly cropped up in my hearing during a family conversation, when I could sense the underlying, unspoken grief, and I felt the embarrassment of an intrusive outsider.

Kenny, the youngest son, caused some amused surprise and amazement in our scattered but close community by having arrived so late in Mrs Squires' life. Needless to say, he was more than somewhat spoilt by his parents and sisters.

Well over sixty years later, I now look back with some pride at my time on the farm. Far from being mundane, it is now part of social history. I saw the last of the corn-binders, still horse-drawn in some instances, ejecting dusty sheaves to be stooked to dry then gathered and ricked, thatched and awaiting the arrival of the thrasher in late autumn. Followed by the straw comber a few weeks later, to sift and refine the remaining straw for use as thatch. We worked late on benign summer days, to get the crop in as eventide stole in under a harvest moon and rabbits shyly appeared. A wraith-like barn owl swooped spectrally across the emerging stars and a temperate breeze carried soft meadow scents to cool our heated bodies.

I turned drying grass with a pitchfork, pared hedges with a billhook and began to learn the rudiments of the art of hedge-steeping; I drove a horse and cart, rolled full milk churns up to the roadside stand for the milk lorry to collect. I knew intimately the small dairy herd, each by name – Ada, Fairy, Molly, Chipperthorn – each a character in her own right; fretful or peevish, neurotic or skittish, gentle and placid. I milked them early morning and late afternoon, tended their calves and changed their straw bedding in winter when they slept overnight in the shippen. Occasionally, on summer nights, I would steal through the soft twilight to their field just to see them content and settled under the stars, chewing their cud, smell the sweet bovine odour and see amorphous steam rising from their body heat. They knew me, so were unconcerned as the night wrapped itself around us, the soft breeze blew under a silver-star-studded sky, and for a moment I felt at one with them and the universe.

I remained on the farm for eighteen months before, bidden by a restless desire and imagination induced by reading *The Coral Island* and *Martin Rattler*, by a Sunday school outing boat trip on the open sea when sparkling blue rollers gently lifted and dipped the old fishing boat under a cloudless sky, I determined to join the navy and see the world.

Early one September morning I had breakfast and walked one last time with Micky across dew-dusted grass to the still mist-shrouded river, before returning to say goodbye to all my family and animals. I walked to the top of the lane, where Dad picked me up in the Dutton's car. We passed down through the tunnel of trees, past the now fading white-painted stone and over the bridge, leaving my childhood behind, and into the future.

About the Author

Allan left school at the age of 15 and worked as a farm labourer until joining the Royal Navy as a naval cook at the age of 16. He served in the RN for twenty-four years, spending some time on ships based on the Far East Station and West Indies Station. Pensioned at 40, he worked as a chef until retirement. He is now aged 82 and a widower, living with his youngest daughter Sarah on the outskirts of Plymouth.

Having always dreamed of being a writer, he now wishes he had knuckled down to it much sooner!

Also from Blue Poppy Publishing

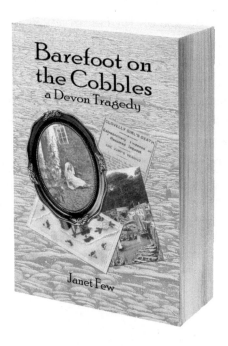

One hundred years ago, in the euphoria of the armistice, a young woman lay dying in a North Devon fishing village. Her parents stood trial for manslaughter. After a century of secrecy, here is the true story of the troubled individuals involved, and the traumas in their past that resulted in tragedy.